The 13th chakra system of ancient Egypt

Sonya Roy

The 13th chakra system of ancient Egypt

The author of this book does not dispense medical advice or prescribe the use of any technique as a form of treatment for physical or medical problems without the advice of a physician, either directly or indirectly. The intent of the author is only to offer information of a general nature to help you in your quest for emotional and spiritual well-being. In the event you use any of the information in this book for yourself, which is your right, the author and the publisher assume no responsibility for your actions.

You can contact the Author through multimedia:

Website:	http://sonyaroy.com/English/
Email:	Sonya@sonyaroy.com
Facebook:	www.facebook.com/reduwellnesscentre/
twitter:	@RoySonyaroy
YouTube:	ReduwellnessCenter
Instagram:	tinaythewarriorprincess
Podcast:	https://sonyaroy.podbean.com

revised date: 2023-11-13

to order additional copies of this book, contact the author.
Category: religion/spirituality- new age spirituality- spiritual
Self-help- personal transformation- spiritual
Health- alternative- meditation

Dedication

To my dear friend Kristine Pel, my dearest supporter who helps me through the long days and is the greatest administrative assistant. Thank you from my whole being!

Table of Contents

INTRODUCTION

It is essential to understand one thing: You are energy. All living things are created by and comprised of energy. The ability of your energy centers to function optimally is what keeps you psychologically, emotionally, physically, and spiritually balanced. The energy is distributed through energy centers known as, "Chakras". There are seven recognized chakras, but that is a limited view of a more complete system that encompasses the entire body. It is also a common belief that the chakras originated from India, more than that, it is a worldwide known system that is described the same way, just with different names. The Egyptians had a system of 13 major chakras and that is the system we will explore in more detail.

We live in a time where science has proven the existence of atoms and radiation, science has even advanced to the point where they have discovered that the atom is not the smallest particle, but that quantum particles are. This may change as science continues to evolve, but the point is there are things that exist beyond what we can see and originally believed. Everything in the world is made of atoms. Just like a cell in your body is made of up to 80% of water, Water is composed of atoms of hydrogen and oxygen joined together (H_2O). Science has discovered that the space occupied by the cell creating water is not empty but filled with an even smaller particle called Quantum. Therefore, we can extend the same logic to the rest of the cell composure your body as the space between any atoms if filled with Quantum energy, so we are made of 100 % energy.

The energy needs to circulate and flow through the body, for your body to work properly. Therefore, it is so important to know how the energy works, to recognize when the energy is blocked or low and how to restore the flow, restoring your energy level to allow your energy distribution to remain open and fully functional.

There are several ways to balance your energy using food, color, sounds, crystals, aroma therapy, and yoga. This will adjust not only your physical body, but your mental body, emotional body, etheric body and your spiritual body.

This book allows for a spiritual connection to be made with the chakras and to teach effective yet simple tools to connect with the subconscious mind to allow a deep profound healing of the soul and not just a shallow clearing of physical symptoms out of the way.

Chapter 1: What are Chakras

Discussions about chakras originated in India around 1,500 B.C., there is also mention of chakras in the, "Yoga Sutras" of Patanjali, dating to circa 200 B.C. However, the West didn't hear much about chakras until the subject was introduced by, Sir John Woodroffe (aka Arthur Avalon), in the early 20th century, it was him that introduced the traditional seven chakras that are positioned throughout your body, from the base of your spine to the crown of your head. There was also, H. P. Blavatsky, who taught the knowledge of the wheels of light, mixed in with Yoga from India. The ideas and concepts were further developed as the 7 chakra system.

Each chakra has its' own vibrational frequency, color, and it governs a specific function that helps make you, in your physical form, but also your emotional, mental, etheric and spiritual bodies which are primarily made of energy. I however, work with the Ancient Egyptian wisdom that describes 13 major chakras, so chakras are not just a Hindu thing, they are universal. In the ancient Egyptian knowledge using 13 chakras, including 2 hearts, one heart of pure love or universal love and one heart relating to the body and emotions, known as Unconditional love. Additional chakras are located on the chin as the way you present yourself to the world and the nose, for focus of intent which is akin to manifestation or affirmations. This area, I attributed to the manifestation center with the nose and chin, joined together.

In order to truly understand how to heal your chakras you first need to understand what they are. Chakras are three-dimensional spinning wheels that distribute energy along the central channel and divide the energy along the different main chakras and each main chakra has a specific color, as I have indicated previously. Chakras are energy distributors just like the electric substation that distribute electricity to your house. The chakras then distribute the energy to the organs, endocrine system, the meridian system where they will help to perform many functions, such as connecting our energy fields, and our bodies to the broader cosmic energy.

The energy is being absorbed from two main points. From the central sun, known as the "Acturius", this is where the higher power resides and from Mother earth who is a conscious being who voluntarily accepted to help with the human soul evolution, in order to develop herself as a third dimensional being. Depending on the culture the energy being absorbed by the central channel has many names. In China, they call it "Chi". For the Japanese, they call it, "Ki". In India, they refer to it as "Prana" and the Native American call it "Orende."

The 13th chakra system of ancient Egypt

There are as many as 122 minor chakras, similar to the major chakras that affect our energy intake and distribution located at the base of the spine, (Base chakra), at the navel, (sacral chakra), in the solar plexus, (solar plexus chakra), within your heart, (heart chakra), within the throat, (throat chakra), at the center of your forehead, (third eye chakra), and at the top of your head, (crown chakra). In the Egyptian knowledge, there are also energy centers, below the feet, (grounding chakra), at the feet, (root chakra), just above the heart, (universal love chakra), at the base of the skull, nose and mouth, (manifesting chakra), and just above the head, (soul star chakra). These chakras are linked together along the central channel, so they directly affect each other. As the energy circulates through the chakras and is inside the chakra, the energy circulates in a clockwise direction. This is usually because a healthy individual uses the energy to power up and live in the moment. However, it is possible to circulate the energy in the opposite direction and deal with past issues. A healthy person is one who lives in a state of balance where the energy is leveled and even, not low or spiking. This energy is contained inside the aura which is explained later on.

Chapter 2: How do we heal the Chakras

The energy flows through the open chakras and regulates all the body's processes, from organ function to the immune system and it is directly affected by emotions and thoughts. The energy is then dispersed through the body's organs and glands. Simply put, blocked energy leads to illness.

In order to heal, we need to open and balance our chakras. There are several techniques that can be used to effectively do this. Among such techniques are rock and crystal healing, aroma therapy, color, sound, vibration, yoga and food. Each technique can be used with a specific chakra.

The chakras can become blocked and when this happens, we feel out of balance or ill. The block may be created on several levels. It could be emotional, mental, or spiritual. After a situation, if the emotions or thoughts are ignored, it will continue to build energy and finally permeate through the physical body which creates a physical manifestation of the issue. If the blockage has been there for a long period of time, we may need professional help from the medical sector. The longer the blockage has been there, the more physical ailments will occur, gradually and unnoticed until we finally need acute medical attention, like cancer.

A chakra can be open, obscured or completely blocked, but in any case, a healthy regime would include regular care of your energy channels. For our chakras to function properly, they must be able to balance the energy through the whole system. Once our energy is balanced, then we can adjust the level of energy we use and share with the world, this will affect our inward and outward flow.

Once a chakra is blocked, you will then need to clear, clean, energize and activate each chakra. You can start with a specific one or you can start at the root and work your way up. Eventually all chakras will need to be looked at, examined and healed.

Rock and crystal healing

Crystal healing is based on the belief that stones or crystals have a natural healing frequency that can be activated to contribute to moving or balancing energy around them. In the case of chakra stones, the vibrational signature of each crystal corresponds or resonates with specific chakras. The crystals or rocks don't need to be large or perfect, just place a crystal on each chakra for the benefit. Different types of crystals will have different energy effectiveness. They take away the bad energy, invigorate the weak chakra and hold positive frequency. The best type of crystal to use for each chakra is referenced later in this book. They can be simple stones or embedded in Jewelry.

A laying down position is ideal for working with chakra crystals. You can also simply hold the crystal in your hand to be beneficial. You may wear it as jewelry, for example a pendant on a necklace, or in a pocket can be used as a shield. You can use any piece of clothing, like a bra, if you prefer to keep it close to your body.

Focus on activating the resonance between the stone and your chakra. Using the power of your intention, meditation, or to simply relax, knowing you have the support of the chakra stones to harmonize frequencies.

It is important to remember, to cleanse or recharge your stones before and after using them. For that, there are many methods including leaving them under water or salt water for a little while but use caution with salt water as some crystals are sensitive to it. Leaving them exposed to the sun is another way to recharge your stones after use, but this may cause some stones to lose their coloring. I recommend utilizing the moonlight for a night, especially during the full moon. You can also smudge them with sage or burying them in the soil for an extended period of time, for more intense regeneration.

Aromatherapy

Aromatherapy has been practiced beneficially to heal for ages. Scents like cedar, cypress tree, hyssop and cinnamon are commonly used. You can also use fresh flowers, or tree bark however, aromatherapy typically involves using oils, made from plants, flowers, roots, fruits and bark, they are quite potent and work well. They are easy to use and completely safe.

Some brands of scented oils use synthetic unnatural fillers that contain very little natural plant derived oil. I recommend taking therapeutic grade Essential oils. Real essential oils will respond through the nose that has thousands of nerve endings and work on the central nervous system. It can also be used through a massage, on clothes, jewelry or in a bath. Different oils help alleviate several symptoms. Certain essential oils will have more than one beneficially useful focus, working congruently on different energy levels. To remain effective, essential oils should be kept in a cool dark area.

Aromatherapy can be used alone, in meditation, and in conjunction with chakra crystals. It can be set in a diffuser at home, in the car, or at the office. Essential oils can also be beneficial when applied directly to your skin, or in specially made jewelry. These oils can come in small bottles and are easy to carry when traveling. Essential oils are an excellent way to stay balanced even in your travels.

Color

Color is important, as they represent different light frequencies and humans need light. A lack of light or trouble absorbing light will cause a person's mind and body to react negatively, such as vitamin deficiencies, hormonal disorders, disturbance of the body's normal patterns, including sleep, metabolic functions and even depression such as Seasonal Affective Disorder.

Our bodies respond to color in food and clothing and our surroundings. But in the end, colors are a form of frequency and by that standard a form of energy. Sounds vary from 20 to 20 000 HZ where light can be measured from 370 trillion to 750 trillion HZ. The human eye can only see a certain range of color and it can expand to x-rays, infra-red, ultraviolet and moves to sound like microwaves or cell waves. White is the presence of all colors, in contrast to black that is not a color but the absence of color.

Each chakra is color specific and color carries a frequency that affects our energy vibrations. Color on your walls, your furniture, your blankets, your clothes all affect your mood, emotional and mental balance. It may include many beautiful decorative objects and colorful images. It may also be worn with accessories such has scarves or jewelry. You can also change your environment by using colored bulbs. A more expensive option is colored ray lamps. You can also wear colored glasses lenses for some time during the day. These chakra energy colors are also an important healing component when you add color to your bath.

Sound and Vibrations

A sound healing practitioner will look at clients from an energy perspective, i.e. their aura or electromagnetic blue print, and seeks to re-balance their clients using sound frequencies, which will correct any vibrational imbalances in their chakra energy system. When an organ in the body is not working at its optimum, its sound pattern will be gone or distorted. With help of sounds we re-introduce the corrected sound frequency pattern that will help heal the chakra, and return it to health, through the law of resonance. This law states that when one energy system encounters another, similar system, their vibrations must come in the state of resonance or harmonic vibration. Why are all these vibrations so important and why do they affect us so much? Because, our body is like an oscillator. We look like a solid mass to the eyes, but we are made of atoms of pure energy forming matter and that energy is directly affected by the wave surrounding it. Your thoughts have a frequency, and your emotions have a frequency, and each specific emotion will have higher vibrations.

Anxiety frequency is felt in the stomach and digestive system and relates to the Solar Plexus. Anger frequency can reverberate through all the chakras, while depression frequency is seated deeply in the manifestation center, 3rd eye and crown.

David R. Hawkins measured frequencies and established a scale:

20	Shame	250	Neutrality
30	Guilt	310	Willingness
50	Apathy	350	Acceptance
75	Grief	400	Reason
100	Fear	500	Love
125	Desires	540	Joy
150	Anger	600	Peace
175	Pride	750 à 1000	Divine; Enlightenment
200	Courage		

Our brain is made up of right and left hemispheres. Both sides need to work together to combine emotions and mental functions. It also connects with the higher consciousness, from the right brain connecting to the spiritual realm and 3rd dimension controlled by the left brain. The right side of the brain is living in the now, connected directly to conscious of the divine. The plants and animals live in the now. They are not slowed down by words, logic or thinking.

Around the world, several countries use music and vibrations to realign a person's energetic vibration. Tibetan use tingshas, (two small bells), to help their meditation by emitting low frequencies, between 4 to 8 Hz, that level is like the brain waves emitted while meditating. They are also able to use sound frequencies from metal bowls to resonate with the chakra and dislodge the elements stuck to your energy fields. They understand the use of sounds combined with intent, can produce miraculous effects on the body and the mind.

Native Americans and several indigenous tribes across the world use sound to conduct their healing energy session such as: Rattles, drums, flutes or their voice. The rhythmic beating of shamanic drumming varies from 0.8 to 5 Hz. Science can now explain why the sounds actually work. The rhythmic stimulation affects the electrical activity of the brain. A single beat of a drum contains many sound frequencies.

The Native American simply explains the power of the drum as the same pulse as mother earth. Which science confirmed since the Schumann resonance is rated at 7.8 Hz. Indigenous people across the globe are the most advanced on the face of the earth in developing inner abilities of healing and understanding of the world they live in, because of that, they are closer in harmony with their surroundings.

In India and in Buddhism, body workers utilize single sounds or Mantras to go deeper into their meditative state. Mantras can help us to quiet our busy minds, so that we can become open to listening, being, and hearing from the Universal Powers. Each chakra has a specific mantra associated to it. You may want to pair up a Japa Meditation with a specific mantra. You can also use more modern tools such as Crystal Bowls. They are made of 99% silica sand (quartz), spun in a centrifugal mold which is heated to 4000 degrees, where an electric arc in the center fuses the individual's grains into one whole. That is why the inside of the bowl is smooth and the external will look and feel granular, with tiny quartz grains. Once fashioned, they come out of the mold, they are then configured in tune. These special music frequency bowls are a great way to reconfigure harmonious vibrations in the body. You can also use tuning forks, the chakras are associated with the musical scale, each note resonates with different chakras. These 13 chakras create a complete musical scale with sharp notes.

Physical Exercise

Yoga can specifically target some chakras, helping open them and letting the energy flow though you. Specific poses are applied to chakras in their individual chapter. Energy Healing such as Reiki is also a great way to balance the chakras along with acupuncture, and Tai Chi. They are not necessarily chakra specific but provide great restoration to energy flow. Another great way to get grounded again is to spend time in nature, Earth Energy can be absorbed by simple walking in nature.

Food

Everywhere in nature, in the growth of trees, plants and herbs there is a multitude of colors. Each plant in nature holds unique energy patterns that can often be broken down to fractal shapes, associated to sacred geometry.

We have lost touch with the real world; we disrespect it because we no longer see its interrelation to us and our survival. We aren't required to fish, hunt or grow our food, we no longer forage like our ancestors did and work hard for our essentials that mother earth used to give us and thus we lack our gratitude in return. When you take something from nature, a rock, crystal, tree branch, leave an offering of Tobacco behind to thank mother earth. Do not take more than you need, keep the land clean, recycle as much as you can.

Nature is the closest ally to the Shaman's natural remedy. Always ask the plant or tree their permission before harvesting them. I did that when I took an Oak Tree seedling from California. It was about 3 inches high and it wanted to come. So, I replanted him here. I later found out the owner was simply yanking them out of the ground as unwanted growth. He's over 6 feet high after only 5 years happily growing in my front yard. He needed to adapt to the cold, but he loves the water and the space.

A healthy diet, clean and vibrant water, and lots of sleep and relaxation are essential to having healthy energetic systems. High ongoing stress creates serious damage in auras and chakras as well as the physical body. A healthy diet also consists of variety and try to eat the food without taking away all its nutrients. Look to specific chapters to see what foods reinforce a chakra's strength and balance.

It is important that you look at your food, eat your food slowly and savor it. Part of the food we choose will be for the vibration they provide, but the color also affects us through our eyes and so the presentation of the food is just as important as the taste.

Ascended Masters

Ascended masters are associated with certain chakras. Rays are the light that shines from the masters, because they are the keepers of certain qualities or energies they transmit through their light. If an ascended master resonates with you, they will gladly help you no matter what color of ray they hold. They are masters and they are dedicated to humanity's growth.

Archangels

The same principle applies to archangels. If you are working closely with one archangel or feel a certain affinity with a specific archangel, then you can continue working with them. But certain Archangels have been associated with certain tasks and work very well with certain chakras. An archangel is an angel of high rank. The word "archangel" itself is usually associated with the Abrahamic religions, but beings that are very similar to archangels are found in a number of religious traditions. Archangels are one of the nine orders of angels that God created to be his messengers. Each of the seven archangels was given special gifts and charged with helping people in a specific way.

Meditation

The benefits of meditation are to provide a state of emotional and physical well-being. The idea is to achieve an ideal state of health by acquiring a peaceful, quiet mind. Meditation helps balance and relax the body, mind and soul. Because the chakras can be influenced by negative thoughts that have the ability to negatively impact the chakras, meditation is an effective energy balancing tool. Other techniques used to support meditation include guided imagery, body relaxation, visualization and breathing techniques. Meditation and conscious breathing are a key to clearing your chakras. By using Energy to cleanse and revitalize your chakra and re-aligning all your bodies around your central channel and your main chakras. You can use my you tube channel to review my Chakra meditation.

The 13th chakra system of ancient Egypt

There is a specific meditation method described in my videos that can be performed to wash each chakra turning left then turning right. As you go through each chakra, visualize cleansing light pouring into them, explore the key points regulated by the chakra and listen to your emotions, feelings, names that come to your mind. As you clear your issues which arise in the past, you create space for energy to fill the chakra and bring it back to the present moment. You should also spend time alone in prayer. Prayer connects us with our Higher Power bringing emotional balance and stability. The power of prayer can be quite amazing. These practices energize and heal our energy systems.

Aura

Aura is present in everything that is alive, a plant, tree, crystals, humans and animals. In healthy humans, it can extend up to 30 feet around you. Your thoughts, your words are also made of the same energy and get projected each time you create them. The same can be said about beliefs, and faith. Auric brushing or having someone run their hands down your aura from top to bottom can help release blockages in your auras. You need to gain awareness of your thoughts, words and actions and see how each affects your energetic fields and therefore acknowledge how they affect your environment. You are a co-creator of the life you live. Change your thoughts, words and actions and you will change the world you live in.

Chapter 3: Sacred Space

Energy clearing is important because of all the interactions we have in a day. We are constantly affected by energy exchanges from public spaces, your residence, personal interactions, your thoughts, and your emotions. One easy way to clear yourself and your space is to use smudge. Smudging can be done with fire clearing and water cleansing. Just like any spiritual work you should not be consuming drugs or alcohol before or during session. It is important that you ground yourself and this can be done through the chakra clearing meditation that helps you move the energy along your central channel into each chakra sinking deep down into mother earth along with some deep breathing.

House Blessing

Before you begin, gather the items you'll need. You will prepare incense, a candle, a lighter or book of matches, Sage but you can also use Frankincense and Myrrh, which are a common combination in their rituals for cleansing spaces, a large feather or fan, and water smudge. Make sure windows are slightly opened in the house. Starting outside, some people like to perform this ritual with a partner or friend while you're walking through this process. While you stand outside to begin the process: Begin with lighting your candle near the front door, it's best to have one inside glass so wind won't blow it out. Close your eyes and imagine a flame being lit within your own body. Walk back to the entrance of the land and place incense just before the entrance on the land. Say your prayer asking your higher power to send light and purify the land and the house.

~ Great Spirits, I (state your name) and (if you have a partner), bring to light this flame of fire, to clear, cleanse and protect my home, and my land from the muck and mire.

Then pick up the smudge or smudge stick and lift it in front of you. Go to the east and as you walk spread the smudge with feather or fan. To the east, call on brother Eagle. Eagle medicine is to help you lift your problems, helps you see the bigger picture and the fine details to achieve your goals. Walk to the corner of the land and plant some incense sticks and walk over to the south, call on brother Coyote. Coyote medicine helps with bringing back laughter, eliminating gossip and helping you communicate better. Walk to the corner of the land and plant some incense sticks and walk over to the West, call on brother Bear. Bear medicine helps with giving you strength and knowing when it's time to work and when it's time to rest. It helps you own your space without having to fight for it. Walk to the corner of the land and plant some incense sticks and walk over to the North, call on brother Buffalo. Buffalo medicine helps with giving vision, establish long term goals, help you look into the future with optimism. Walk to the corner of the land and plant some incense sticks and walk over to the front door.

Before you enter the house, spray the door frame with the water smudge. Go in and bringing the candle with you and place it in the main room, and light lavender incense to burn during the house clearing. Allow the smoke from the sage to permeate each room. Imagine the smoke clearing out the energies around you replacing it with clear bright white light from the divine forces. Begin facing East and walk clockwise, fanning the smoke as you go. You again call unto Animal medicine of eagle, coyote, bear and buffalo. Keep the function of the room in mind.

For example:

Bedroom:
Brother eagle help lift my worries and give me vision in my personal life. Brother coyote bring clear messages to me in my dreams. Brother bear allow me to relax, and rest easy at night. Brother buffalo give me vision in my dreams and let me see what message is sent to me by my higher self.

Kitchen:
Brother eagle lift clouds and ambiguity and let me see the details of my life while maintaining my life purpose. Brother coyote help me with clear communication and humor and remove temptation to gossip. Brother bear help me be healthy in my choices and avoid temptation. Brother buffalo help me envision the future and plan my meals.

As you pass a window allow the energy within the home to move out into the world where it can be dissipated and no longer do harm or affect others again.

Spray the frame of each door before entering the room, do the same thing around each window sill. After the room is smudged in all directions, close the window. This is a symbolic gesture locking in your protection.

As you reach the last room of the house complete the process by saying:

(your higher power), I bring blessing to this home, to bring forth happiness and joy, to provide security and abundance, to share in love, friendship and laughter. Free any spirits attached to this house or the objects inside the house or the land and allow them to enter your light and be release from their earthly bounds. To close the ceremony, spend a few minutes focusing on the land, the house and see each room filled with light and the entire dwelling be surrounded by a large egg of golden light. You can use this time to thank your higher power that has helped you. Blow out the candle.

You may want to make the land yours and thank mother earth for her protection and blessing, a rose bush would be an appropriate gift but planting anything will work, if you live in condo or apartment get a plant. Raise the unplanted bush or plant and present it to the divine forces. Say something like this:

(Your higher power) I give thanks of rose and thorn as my symbol of gratitude and honor.
to Mother Earth who's light and love shall shine through its petals of beauty, to remind us all of your unselfish gifts. So be it.

Sacred Space

In your sacred space, you should have all your tools readily available such as a pen, journal, sage, water, your crystals, and a candle. The candle represents the light you are asking creator to send to you. For sacred space, clearing and cleansing should be done before each use. This can be done within a minute or two, you don't have to make this a major effort. If you don't have sage, you can also use incense. You need to have a sacred space, a space dedicated to your mediation and healing work. You can simply light a candle and burn sage around the room and walking in a clockwise direction to move out negative and unwanted energies, let the smoke brush against the walls and the objects in the room. After you can use a water bottle that has dried cedar in it and spray the area, to set a shield to keep those energies from re-entering the space. This is very much the equivalent of passing a broom and after wards washing the floors. Although the broom removed the large pieces and excess off the floor, the floor was not completely clean until it was washed with water. You then want to energize your space with the help of extra energy. You can call on your higher power and ask for your space to be bathed in light. For those of you who practice energy work, you can fill the room or space with energy. See the house clearing, and repeat the room clearing steps.

Throughout the book, I will provide Ascended Masters to work with and Archangels, don't be afraid to ask for their help. If you are familiar with an Archangel and Ascended master feel free to call on them for help. Ask for protection of the space and for the information to come only for the highest good for the person seeking help, create an auric shield to protect yourself from your low energy, or energy leak and keep you strong during your healing work. For those of you who can see energy, it will take the form of a golden egg big enough to surround you and your sacred space.

Water smudge

Purchase a small bottle of Rose oil (about 2 ounces), and a larger glass container to hold a little mixture you're going to have to make. You can get these from your local craft store. When you get home, pour half the contents of the rose oil into the bottle. Tear up 4 or 5 rose petals and add them to the bottle. Boil some tap water and fill up the bottle. Now you have a quick water smudge.

New acquisitions

Any new object you have made or purchased should always be cleansed before use. Additionally, it's common to empower the object with a specific energy for its intended use. For instance, you may find a rose quartz crystal that you want to use for emotional healing. This crystal should be consecrated with that specific intent and only used for that purpose. This is true for any object or tool you use for spiritual work, be it a wand, crystals, instrument and even candles used in your sacred space. The best time to clear, cleanse and consecrate new tools or objects is right after their purchase. The energy from the New Moon heightens the clearing and cleansing of new objects, but it's also good for re-cleansing and re-programming objects. You can use other tools that you have already empowered with specific uses to help you clear, cleanse and even consecrate a new object.

When you clear your tools such as crystal, wands, or musical instruments, you can give them a purpose. To a crystal you express your intent with a prayer such as: "God/Goddess, I ask your assistance to charge this crystal with the light and energy of the divine, with unconditional love and the knowledge of understanding, for the purpose of clearing, cleansing and energizing this gift." or "I receive this beautiful (name the object) with appreciation and thanks. I ask the divine forces present to help me clear, cleanse and consecrate this object for the use of (state the purpose again).

The 13th chakra system of ancient Egypt

This is another way, "I use the smoke of this sage & cedar (or whatever) to cleanse the old from this gift. To move out any previous energy that exists within its walls either by purpose or by accident." Or, "I ask the God/Goddess to take the negative energies from this object/proxy and move it out into the universe where it can be dissipated and no longer do harm to any one, not to me, those who meet this object/proxy from now to the future, through the life of the object/proxy. I ask that the energies placed on this object prior to this day, whether by intent or by accident, be removed and dissipated."

To conclude the ceremony, close your eyes and thank God/Goddess for coming to your aid and guiding your energy and words. You can say, "I thank all the forces who came for their assistance, I ask that the energy of this object be closed for the purpose of this cleansing and re-energizing. I ask that only that which is still needed within my home, my being and the object/proxy remain until such time as the divine energy has affected the positive changes desired. I bless thee and thank thee all. Amen"

Personal Energy

Finally, you should regularly clear and cleanse your own energy. Every contact you make carries its own frequency and affects our own. It doesn't have to be a close friend, it can simply be a bus driver or a plant or animal you met along the way. Regular clearing of your energy will help you achieve mental, physical and emotional clarity. You can say "I welcome (the name of the person) into my circle with honor and respect. I ask the divine forces present to help us clear, cleanse and rejuvenate their energies of mind/body and spirit for the purpose of (whatever they need, health, a special meeting coming up and so on)."

Mental clarity will help you in your life because it is present in everything that you do. You first think about it and then set into motion. There are no actions that are not affected by our thought's first, we are simply operating on a more subconscious level but still thoughts, are required and affect all our daily activities such as cooking, gardening, needlework, studying, hiking, or many other different types of activities. Your mental body needs to be stimulated, learn new things and be challenge or stimulated. We need to be learning, interested, and passionate about something at all times in our lives. As the adage goes, if you don't use it, you will lose it.

Physical clarity is the most elusive one because in our society we learn to mask our symptoms the second we feel a discomfort. We mask the messages we receive and ignore the warnings. We keep pushing, working more hours, pushing our system beyond its ability to cope and then we cover the other symptoms with stronger medications. Physical clarity means that you live in harmony with your body, you respect your limit and recognize that limits do not make you weak. You live in harmony with your environment and are able to create space for balanced healthy choices.

Emotional clarity helps you express your emotions to others, with a balanced system you can do so with compassion and love. It allows you to give and receive love from family, friends and community are important. While you clear your energy with smudge and water smudge, make your intent clear, you might state something like, "Clear and cleanse me in order for divine purpose and energies to enter my life and help me with the mission and lessons in this life". You can refer to the smudging video on YouTube. http://www.SonyaRoy.com.

Chapter 4: Base Chakra

The knowledge gathered here is based on exhaustive research from western publications and more esoteric information from the ancient Egyptians, Tibetan books, and Indian books. The central theme of base chakra in the Egyptian System or more commonly known as the root chakra is the energy center that is associated with your most basic survival needs. It relates to family matters, early childhood, financial matters, parental issues, physical identity, and is oriented to self-preservation. The base draws its energy from the ground and roots the body and soul to the earth. It is related to the most basic of needs, such as instinct, security, survival, and human potential. Ideally this chakra brings us health, prosperity, security, and dynamic presence.

The root chakra is located in the feet. The base chakra is located at the base of the spine, for the rest of the book when I refer to the root chakra, I refer to the feet.

Basics of the Base Chakra

Location	At the base of the spine. It corresponds to the perineum
Energy	Yin
Element	Earth
Mantra	LAM (pronounced LANG), or I am.
Sound	C note, 400 to 484 cycles per seconds or hertz.
Organs	It mostly represents the sexual organs.
Spine	It encompasses the first three vertebrae at the pelvic plexus.
Endocrine System	Ovaries, testis, controls sexual development and secretes sex hormones.
Color	RED and can take on various shades depending on the energy level of the chakra.

The Main Functions:

The themes for the Base chakra are safety, grounding, right to live, security, and money. Everything that has to do with survival, preservation of self and vital needs.

The 13th chakra system of ancient Egypt

The Base chakra provides the foundation on which we build our life. It supports us in growing and feeling safe into exploring all aspects of life. It is related to our feelings of safety and security, whether it's physical regarding our bodily needs or metaphorical regarding housing and financial safety. To sum it up, the first chakra questions are around the idea of survival and safety.

Unbalanced Chakra

The unbalanced chakra would present a multitude of symptoms depending on whether the symptoms are coming through the physical, emotional, mental, or spiritual body. Rather than referring to ourselves as sick or stuck with an illness, we need to start recognizing that it is unbalanced energy that creates the sickness. We are not sick, it's that we are not balanced. The imbalance represents itself in multiple forms depending on which of the bodies it lies in.

Physical:

Symptoms may include a lack of control, such as being overweight or trying to control something through anorexia or bulimia. It also presents itself as fatigue, lower back pain, sexual dysfunction, restlessness, blood disorder, menstrual issues, yeast infections, and prostate or rectal issues ranging from blockage to cancer.

Etheric:

This body holds memories or programming you have become accustomed to through your faith, your family, and your culture. Your memories are stopping you from advancing and becoming secure in your life, your finances, and your body. This relates entirely to your belief system, and like anything else, it can become unbalanced. You might have been brought up to think a man can hit you, or that you have no say if someone wants to have a sexual relationship with you, or that you cannot succeed on your own and need to rely on others to provide for you.

Mental:

The person will present a fear of lack in the form of avarice and greed and constantly be living in survival mode. A person with an unbalanced chakra does not have the faith that universe will take care of them. The person can be excessively negative and critical. They will feel they have no control over their thoughts, and that leads to poor decision making.

Emotional:

The person may feel angry, short tempered, belligerent, impatient, unusually aggressive, insecure, or anxious. A person may have tendencies to gamble. They are in constant mode of survival and never feel safe.

Spiritual:

The person often feels ungrounded, spacey, and lost in thoughts. It is the root for addictions (sexual, alcohol, narcotics, food, gambling, etc.) in other words, if you have an addiction, your chakra is unbalanced.

Healing Your Base Chakra

The Base chakra is at the base of the line of traditional chakras. If your Base chakra is unbalanced or completely blocked this does not mean that all your chakras are in the same position. But an imbalanced chakra does affect the circulation of energy overall, so it is important to look at each chakra and determine how each one is affected.

Consider if you recognize some of the symptoms listed in this chapter, and then refer to chapter 2 to use the techniques to dissolve any blockages before continuing on with other chakras. It is important to focus your time and energy on doing one chakra right, rather than trying to fix everything all at once. Healing one chakra completely will also reinforce the others by providing a greater supply of energy and a better circulation throughout the body. Remember, the method of healing is the same for all chakras, but the specific stone, smell, food, or yoga posture will differ.

You don't need to use all the methods sited in chapter 2, because, for example, you may not know yoga or physically be ready to practice yoga, but you can use aroma therapy or crystals to start. To re-balance a chakra, it is not required or needed to use all the methods below, but you have a wide variety to choose from. Simply select one that agrees with your life style.

To start, you can simply engage in grounding activities that help you connect to nature, such as gardening, walking, or hiking. It's important that you feel safe in your environment, so perhaps have a plant close by.

Aroma therapy:

You should consider using earthly scents from essential oils such as cedar, cloves, cypress, myrrh, patchouli, rosemary, sandalwood or ylang-ylang.

Food:

You can help balance the Base chakra by adding naturally red-colored food, such as beets or strawberry. Also add root vegetables, such as parsnips, carrots, and potatoes. The Base chakra can also be balanced by eating soy, tofu, eggs, and beans which are all a good source of protein. Spices such as ginger and sweet flag are also grounding.

Rocks & Crystals:

Color:
Red colored crystals and stones are associated with the Base chakra, such as :

Cinnabrite, Garnet, Hessonite, Red Carnelian, Red Jasper, Red Tiger Eye, Sunstone, Tiger Iron

Frequency:
Or they can be identified by frequencies:

Agate Black Banded, Black Sapphire, Blue Tiger Eye, Champagne Aura Quartz, Chrysoberyl, Chrysoprase, Citrine, Cobalto Calcite, Copper, Crocoite, Dalmatian Jasper, Desert Rose, Diamond, Dioptase, Emerald, Fire Agate, Gold Quartz, Green Aventurine, Green Calcite, Green Tourmaline, Hematite, Infinite, Jet, Morganite, Moss Agate, Mystic Topaz, Nephrite Jade, Orange Calcite, Petalite, Picasso Marble, Preseli Bluestone, Pyrite, Ruby, Sardonyx, Serpentine, Shiva Lingam, Smokey Quartz, Sulfur, Tangerine Quartz, Tiger Eye, Titanium Rainbow Aura Quartz, Vanadinite

Yoga: You are looking at the basic asanas such as :

• Standing forward bend • Uttanasana
• Garland • yogi squat • Malasana
• Head-to-knee forward bend • Janu sirsasana
• Reclining bound angle • Supta baddha konasana

The 13th chakra system of ancient Egypt

• Wide-legged forward bend • Prasarita padottanasana
• Warrior II • Virabhadrasana II
• Lying tree • Standing tree
• Wind-relieving pose • Pavanamuktasana

Meditation:

Meditation to open your base chakra can be done with Alchemy Crystal Bowl. While being played you will be re-aligning the vibration of the body to reach a state of balance. You can also utilize Tibetan bowls or bells to create the same effect. YouTube possesses several free meditations with bowls if you do not own any bowls. During your meditation you can start placing your hands in yoga position called Mudras. This form of yoga is associated with hand placement to stimulate and generate an electric current in a specific chakra.

For the base chakra you can utilise the **Gyan Mudra** formation. This position is to simply join the thumb and index together and to leave the other fingers open, hands resting on the knees.
There is also **Abhaya Mudra** or Fearlessness: Hold right hand slightly cupped at shoulder height, palm facing outward. Allow right elbow to fall close to the waist.

Prithivi Mudra or Centering: Extending both arms outward, touch the tip of the thumbs to the tips of the ring fingers. Allow the other fingers to extend straight out, palms facing up. Rest the backs of the hands-on thighs, knees or in the lap.

Pranidhana Mudra or Surrender: Bringing the hands together, connect the tips of the index and pinky fingers. Curl the middle and ring fingers in to touch the thumb tips. Rest the hands in front of the belly, wrists on thighs.

Ascended Master:

Seraphis Bey is traditionally associated with the Base chakra and known to bring joy, purity, and discipline. You can also call on Lakshmi, The green man, and Hina.

Archangel:

Literature associates either Archangel Gabriel and Archangel Hope to the base chakra.

Kundalini:

Kundalini is known as Qi and is all part of the energy system called Microcosmic Orbit. Kundalini is the female energy that lays dormant and coiled until it is awakened and travels up through all the chakras, rising and channeling the energy. This raising of energy plays a pivotal role in spiritual awakening. It represents an awakening, but beyond that it is when the energy moves through us and through all the chakras. It is represented like a snake as it weaves the energy in and out of chakras in a pattern that resembles the way a snake moves. It starts at the Base chakra and weaves through each chakra center all the way up to the crown. This energy movement helps to balance the chakra centers and keep all five bodies balanced. Mistakenly referred to as sexual energy, it is simply energy moving and linking the different chakras to one another. It is also a balanced energy that contains both male and female, each traveling in opposite directions and meeting at the center of each chakra as they travel up and down through all the five bodies, not just the physical one.

Below are some examples of how kundalini can be used for specific themes, such as sexuality, finances, and humanity's growth.

Sexual Kundalini:

Here the sexual energy is primal and has a main purpose of reproduction and pure satisfaction of physical desires without further involvement. This is not rape, look to mother nature. The female selects the male who competes for the privilege of reproducing, but the female picks the male who has the best chances for her litter to survive and adapt. An example of kundalini stuck in the Base chakra would represent itself as a one-night stand, an empty physical act with no emotional ties. It is a sexual interaction limited to sexual desires but not bestial in nature, so it does not represent rape or lack of free choice between the partners.

Financial Kundalini:

If the kundalini is stuck in the Base chakra it can manifest in a person stuck in survival mode. Where is my rent money coming from? How will I pay my bills? How can I eat? How can I meet my basic needs? The person constantly worries about basic needs being met.

Humanity's Kundalini:

Humanity as a whole takes a lot longer to grow and learn. A lesson needs to permeate the entire subconscious of each soul to become active and move on to the next chakra. Think of it as the beginning of humanity, where we started off as cave men, always looking for food, lodging, and protection, with our lives constantly at risk.

Chapter 5: Sacral Chakra

The 2nd chakra is half way between the survival preoccupations of the Base chakra and the expression of will of the solar plexus chakra. This chakra is the center of our emotions. It supports personal expansion and the formation of identity through relating to others and to the world.

Basics of the Sacral Chakra

Location	It is located under belly button, about 2 or 3 inches below the navel in the lower abdomen.
Energy	Yang
Element	Water, the sacral chakra is associated with the water element, characterized by flow and flexibility of our thought and emotions.
Mantra	VAM or I feel.
Sound	D note, 484 to 508 Hz
Organs	Bladder, prostate, kidneys, gall bladder, bowel, spleen. It is associated with the lymphatic system.
Spine	It's located at the level of the lumbar vertebrae.
Endocrine System	Adrenal glands that regulate the immune system and metabolism
Color	Orange

The Main Functions:

This is where we connect to the outside world. It is our ability to accept others and new experiences. It connects us to others through feeling, desire, sensation, and movement. When the sacral chakra is balanced, you feel in harmony with life. You are able to express yourself creatively and to mature with each new experience life offers, good or bad.

This chakra is also the center of the search for pleasure, whether sensual or through your daily life experiences. We live life through the senses, whether it's auditory, through taste, touch, or sight, which governs basic emotional needs, sexuality, creativity and expression.

A balanced sacral chakra allows you to experience intimacy and love freely and fully, to be honest and non-judgmental about your desires, and to live as your authentic self without fear.

This chakra is also about resourcefulness, utilizing the environment, family & friends, and our creativity to reach our goals. This is done in a respectful way, where everyone benefits, and the exchange is balanced.

Unbalanced Chakra:

This chakra is based on exchange and relationship with the outside world. Therefore, an unbalanced chakra would represent itself as a lack or inability to interact with others or a lack or loss of creativity. It also means you lost the balance between what you take and what you give or contribute. You may feel like you've lost control of your life and can't get traction again.

Physical:

Here are some physical indications that there is an issue with the sacral chakra. Any issues with sexuality. That it is a lack of sexual desire or satisfaction or a sexual obsession. One indicates an overactive chakra while the other indicates an under-active chakra. Physical illness related to the organs energized by the sacral chakra such as a urinary or bladder infections, constipation, infertility, ectopic pregnancies or multiple miscarriages, premenstrual syndrome, anemia, hypoglycemia (low blood sugar), lower back pain, impotence, spleen and kidney issues.

Etheric:

As your etheric body holds the memory of your feelings, if you lose touch with yourself, you may feel numb, out of touch with yourself.

Mental:

To be mentally out of touch with the real world leads you to live in fantasies and losing your ability to be creative. Our lack of connection prevents you from coping with changes in your life. On a more psychological level a person may be dependent or co-dependent or in an unhealthy, and sometimes abusive relationship. A person may appear arrogant but simply feel a detachment or manipulate the environment or a person for their own satisfaction.

Emotional:

Anxiety and fear are present in any chakra that is unbalanced. In the sacral chakra the anxiety comes from feeling stuck in a particular feeling or mood, mania, aggressiveness that does not seem your own. Fear in the sacral chakra represents itself as self-sabotage, or fear of happiness or pleasure. This may lead to impotence or frigidity in women.

You may experience the emotions more strongly than usual, have severe mood swings, or seemingly thrive on conflict and drama that leads to poor personal boundaries. This may lead a person to jealousy as they cannot trust anyone around them. To envy others also represents a sense that we are not satisfied, that our needs are not met. If your emotions are out of proportion for the situation, try to be aware of the situation and balance your emotions.

If you realized that your emotions are out of proportion with the situation, try to become conscious of the situation and start working on a more responsible and appropriate behavior. This is the time to re-balance your emotions.

Spiritual:

The spiritual body is affected by a blocked sacral chakra by the inability to create connections with mentors, teachers and the rejection of spiritual ideas based on anger and false judgments It closes your mind to new ideas, new concepts that could help you grow in your faith and your soul.

Healing Your Sacral Chakra

First and foremost, to heal your chakra is to heal the flow of emotions, keeping them balanced and consistent with the situation. To start, you can simply engage in water activities. For the Base chakra, we needed earth to help us ground. Here we need water, being near open water like lakes, rivers, streams or the ocean. If possible, touch the water, if you cannot swim in it, at least let your feet touch the water so it can absorb the energy. Most cities have water parks, but if this is difficult to access, you can simply take a bath or a shower. This is a time to get in touch with the world around you by getting in touch with friends or family, participate in a team sport, or take a class. The best way to balance your sacral chakra is to get connected again.

Another simple and effective way to engage your sacral chakra is to wear the color orange as a piece of clothing, accessory or a piece of jewelry. Add the color to your home décor, or office.

Aroma therapy:

The scents to consider balancing the sacral chakra are bergamot, cardamom, citrus, clary sage, jasmine, orange, patchouli, rose, sandalwood, ylang-ylang.

Food:

Vegetables: that are of the orange variety will help the sacral chakra balance itself as well. you can choose between carrots, orange pepper, pumpkin, butternut squash, sweet potato

Fruits: You can choose from oranges, melons, coconuts and other sweet fruits such as mangoes, peaches, nectarines, apricots and pineapple.

Spices: Coriander, cinnamon, caraway seed, carob, fennel, sesame seed.

Rocks & Crystals:

Based on color:
Amber, Carnelian, Chiastolite, Copper, Crocoite, Fire Agate, Fire Opal, Halite, Orange calcite, Picasso marble, Pietersite, Sunstone.

The 13th chakra system of ancient Egypt

Frequency:

Apache Tear, Black Banded Agate, Champagne Aura Quartz, Cinnabrite, Garnet, Golden Topaz, Gray Banded Agate Green Calcite, Iolite, Malachite, Moonstone, Olivine, Prehnite, Preseli Bluestone, Shiva Lingam, Snowflake Obsidian, Sulfur, Tiger Eye, Titanium Rainbow Aura Quartz, Unakite, Yellow Jasper, Yellow Mookaite
.

Yoga:

This chakra yoga practice should be slow and relaxed rather than fast or overly challenging such as:

• Reclining bound angle pose • Supta Baddha Konasana
• Half frog pose • Ardha Bhekasana
• Wide-angle seated forward bend • Upavistha Konasana
• Cow face • Gomukhasana
• One-legged king pigeon • Eka Pada Rajakapotasana
• Bound angle • Baddha Konasana
• Revolved triangle • Parivrtta Trikonasana
• Full boat • Paripurna Navasana
• Chair • Utkatasana
• Side plank • Vasisthasana
• Half moon • Ardha Chandrasana
• Goddess • Utkata Konasana
• Crocodile • Makarasana
• Fire log pose • Agnistambhasana

Meditation:

Meditating on the color orange is another great way to not only heal and activate the sacral chakra, but also improves your focus and concentration by envisioning an orange lotus or orange moon or ball in the sacral chakra. Hold that image in your mind for a few minutes while breathing deeply.

You can also journal your emotions as a means of exploration, to find the origins, the seat of your emotions. You ask yourself what is attracted to me? What disgusts me? How does it guide the way you live your life? How attractive do you feel? Are you confident about your self-image or do you judge yourself based on outside influences? Do you feel ruled by your emotions? Are your emotions balances with what provokes them? Are you often indulging in life's little pleasures to the point of losing balance (obsession)? Do you feel selfish for enjoying a treat or when you buy yourself something? Do you know what your passion is in life? Are you able to express it? Are you feeling numb or awake?

During the meditation continue working on your hand position

Dhyani Mudra Rest the back of your right hand in the palm of the other with tips of thumbs lightly touching.
Mira Mudra or Nourishment: Join the tips of the thumbs to the tips of the pinkies on the same hand. Bring the joined fingers and thumbs of head hand to touch at the tips. Extend other fingers up and join the tips of the ring fingers together. Allow hands to rest in lap just below the navel.
Trimurta Mudra or Harmony: Hold hands in front of the pelvis facing downward. Touch the thumbs tips together and connect the index fingers to form a triangle. Rest the hands on the lap, palms facing inward.
Matsya Mudra or Fluidity: Place the right palm over the back of the left hand, both hands facing downward. Keep all of the fingers stacked while extending the thumbs out to the side. Hold hands with fingers extending outward away from the abdomen.

Ascended Master:

Ascended master Isis, Pallas Athena, White Tara

Archangel:

Archangel Metatron, Jophiel and Gabriel.

Kundalini

Kundalini is ever evolving and trying to ascend to the crown. It does follow the chakra energy and our evolution in our five bodies (physical, etheric, mental, emotional and spiritual). The kundalini will not be able to grow if our chakra is blocked. The examples below display a healthy, balanced example of a rising kundalini.

Sexual Kundalini:

Here the sexual energy is evolving from a one-night stand to a relationship. We are seeking a connection as opposed to simple minded sex and immediate satisfaction in exchange for a long-term balance exchange and meeting each other need.

Financial Kundalini:

The sacral chakra is about relationships and desires. The financial kundalini evolves into using our resources either money or services not to the sole satisfaction of our desires but for our community. The money or resources can be exchanged or bartered or donated for the enjoyment of others. Someone donating land to ensure a park will always be there, or someone participating in a food drive and sharing their food are excellent examples.

Humanity's Kundalini:

Humanity as a whole takes small steps with great examples and teachers. As the knowledge is known, the kundalini of humanity raises up. The speed at which we learn has evolved greatly since our humble beginnings. However, it took a long time for us to learn to live as a community and get rid of our fears of lack. We eventually realized that food goes bad fast and perhaps its best to share with a group and when they have food, they will share with us. There was a great leap of trust to be taken, we had to believe that we would get support when we needed it. It became easier to share by living in close proximity and so villages were built. It also became easier to let better hunters hunt and better fisherman fish. This created a place of sharing where everyone had enough food. This also helped in sharing knowledge and build better residences. The extra manpower allowed for progress to be made, afforded better protection and a lot less worry. Eventually, this created a surplus that was exchanged for seed or herbs that were hard to find in certain areas and diversified the food source.

Chapter 6: Solar Plexus Chakra

The solar plexus is our identity center, it is the essence of what makes you unique. This is the point where your self-esteem grows, your will, your discipline, your personal power, your social self, your courage, self-confidence. This chakra can power you to move forward, to reach further, outside the box to realize your intentions and desires.

Basics of the Solar Plexus Chakra

Location	Between the breastbone and a few inches above the naval in the upper abdomen
Energy	**Yin**
Element	**Fire** for its connection to the great central sun, to the flame of our soul, our vital energy and the eternal flame.
Mantra	RAM or I can.
Sound	E note, 508 to 526 Hz
Organs	Liver, stomach.
Spine	T5 to T9
Endocrine System	Pancreas
Color	Yellow

The Main Functions:

This is the seat of empowerment, what is born of your curiosity then feeds your personal interests to discover your sense of self.

A balanced solar plexus leaves the individual feeling centered, with clear goals and objectives. You are autonomous and effective and especially non-dominating in your power. You use your power for you and not to take advantage of anyone else.

This is a great center to bring the changes in your life that will make you happy because it helps determine who you are, what you like, what you are good at, therefore guides you towards the optimal you. It governs impulse control and keeps the ego in check.

Unbalanced Chakra

An unbalanced solar plexus presents itself in a person who lost their strength, lost their sense of identity, this can take multiple forms in the different bodies. This loss can present itself as a person who has no idea who they are and are lifeless or as a person whose central preoccupations are social and empty of purpose. The focus being lost on a false outward image, that does not reflect who the individual truly is.

Physical:

In the body, a person will present with liver issues, bile, ulcers or other digestive problems such has cramps, acidity, gastritis, gallbladder stones, heartburn, eating disorders, insomnia, difficulty to meditate, stress, failing memory.

Etheric:

The memory held by the etheric body is who you are and who you need to be in order to achieve your soul's purpose. This is where a person loses their sense of self and they are unable to decide about their life that it is about relationship, career or personal development. They are stuck.

Mental:

A person would present excessive stubbornness, desire for control of environment and people, perfectionist, be overly critical, manipulative, and misuse their power for their own advantage. A person would be unable to make decisions or put their energy to realizing their dreams. They are insensitive, suspicious, calculating and judgmental.

Emotional:

The person would present as a shy or introverted person with anger issues who are unable to acknowledge their truth, feeling helpless, selfish and irresponsible , afraid to lose control or be controlled, severe insecurities.

Spiritual:

The person is unable to find balance in asserting their personal power and controlling others. They have no ambition and lack purpose. They have no clear identity and are all ego, no soul.

Healing Your Solar Plexus Chakra
To start, you can simply take a class, develop a talent, do something for yourself.

Aroma therapy:

Anise, black pepper, cardamom, chamomile, cinnamon, clove, coriander, cypress, ginger, grapefruit, juniper, lavender, lemon, lemongrass, lime, mandarin, neroli, rosemary, spearmint.

Food:

Fruits:
Lemons, pineapple, yellow apples, yellow figs, yellow kiwi, yellow pears, yellow watermelon, yellow tomatoes.

Vegetables:
Beets, rutabagas, summer squash, turnips, winter squash, yellow and sweet potatoes, yellow peppers.

Other: Brown rice, oats, spelt, olive oil, chamomile, coriander, millet, quinoa, ginger, turmeric, rosemary, sage and thyme.

Rocks & Crystals:

Based on color:
Amber, Ametrine, Citrine, Fire Opal, Golden Calcite, Gold Quartz, Golden Danburite, Golden Fluorite, Golden Healer Quartz, Golden Topaz, Heliodor, Hessonite, Picasso marble, Pyrite, Rainbow Onyx, Sunshine Aura Quartz, Tangerine Aura Quartz, Tangerine Quartz, Schalenblende, Septarian, Sulfur, Tiger Eye, Yellow Jade, Yellow Jasper, Yellow Mookaite.

Frequency:
Anhydrite, Aragonite, Azurite, Beryl, Black Jasper, Bloodstone, Blue Goldstone, Blue Onyx, Blue Opal, Blue Quartz, Blue Sapphire, Blue Tigers Eye, Blue Topaz, Carnelian, Chiastolite, Chlorite Phantom, Chrysoberyl, Chrysoprase, Crocoite, Dalmatian Jasper, Desert Rose, Diamond, Dragon Blood, Dumortierite, Erythrite, Fire Agate, Garnet, Green Aventurine, Grey Jasper, Iolite, Labradorite, Lithium Quartz,

Meteorite, Milky Quartz, Mookaite, Moonstone, Mount Shasta Serpentine, Mystic Topaz, Nirvana Quartz, Nuummite, Ocean Jasper, Olivine, Opal, Opalite, Orange Calcite, Pietersite, Pink Opal, Preseli Bluestone, Rainbow Fluorite, Red Aventurine, Red Mookaite, Red Tiger Eye, Rhodochrosite, Rose Aura Quartz, Rose Quartz, Rutilated Quartz, Sardonyx, Serpentine, Smokey Quartz, Snowflake Obsidian, Staurolite, Sunstone, Tanzanite, Tiger Iron, Titanium Rainbow Aura Quartz, Turquoise, Unakite, Violet Flame Opal, White Calcite

Yoga:

Yoga for the solar plexus includes the following poses:

• Full boat pose • Paripurna Navasana
• Firefly pose • Tittibhasana
• Bharadvaja's twist • Bharadvajasana I
• Warrior 1 • Virabhadrasana I
• Warrior 2 • Virabhadrasana II
• Reverse plank • Purvottanasana
• Bow • Dhanurasana

Meditation:

Your meditation focus should be on you, what are your dreams, what are your gifts what can you do, what are you good at, what can you contribute to our society and make it a better place. Focus on a flame, or a candle and see the power in the fire, let it light your inner strength and power. Embrace your power and use it for the good of humanity. Embrace all that you can be and wash away doubt and fears that you are not enough.

The 13th chakra system of ancient Egypt

For the hands position while meditating you may choose amongst the following:

Hakini Mudra: Rest the back of your right hand in the palm of the other with tips of thumbs lightly touching.
Mushtika Mudra: with each hand, curl the fingers inward, bringing the pads of the fingers towards the palms, thumbs on the outside. Bring the heels of the hands together and join the second joints of the fingers. Extend the two thumbs and bring together. Hold hands lightly against your abdomen.
Surya Mudra: Bend the ring finger of each hand and bring the thumbs. Cover the nail of the ring finger with the pad of the thumb. Extend the remaining fingers. Rest hands on the thighs, palms facing upward.
Shiva Linga Mudra: Place the left palm facing upward in front of the belly. Make a fist with the right hand with the thumb facing up. Place in the center of the left palm.
Matangi Mudra: Interlace the fingers of both hands with right thumb over the left thumb. Extend the middle fingers straight out with the pads of the two fingers touching. Rest the base of the wrists into the solar plexus just where the ribs meet.

Ascended Master:

Ascended Master Lady Nada and Lord Sananda for peace, service and brotherhood.

Archangel:

Archangel Uriel and Aurora

Kundalini

The energy rises from a center of community to an energy that is represented by individuality. This shift occurs when a person although part of a community practices their gifts, talents and become expert or are recognized for their particular contribution.

Sexual Kundalini:

The sexuality evolves into a specific need and individuality, what pleases one partner may not necessarily please another. It is also when as an individual we are free to explore our sexual orientation, taste without shame that we can truly embrace who we are. We find ways to express our individuality through our sexuality and pleasure.

Financial Kundalini:

The solar plexus helps a person build a budget to sustain their needs, but also individualize their spending to help develop their gifts or talents or to further their learning in their career or art. Their individuality also helps them determine how they should earn their money. Some countries have made it possible for their citizens to attend advanced schooling for free, realizing that it was better to have a motivated poor doctor as opposed to a rich person who has chosen medicine simply because it pays well, and their family could pay their school fees.

Humanity's Kundalini:

This phase of humanity came early on as certain people developed their crafts such as tanner, smith or the making of clothes, furniture. Although, it was originally who had a certain talent that would be trained in a particular craft in a tribe where everyone was looked after. Things regressed in the dark ages when the son of a tanner became a tanner not because it was his calling but because he was forced to do so. During the Renaissance period in history, art was again appreciated and celebrated. What remains as a challenge to this day, is to earn a living not because it brings prestige and lots of money but because it responds to your soul calling.

Chapter 7: Double Heart Chakra

The Egyptian believed that there are two Heart Chakras. The one everyone knows about, the Unconditional Love Chakra and the Universal Love Chakra. Let's start with the Unconditional Love Chakra.

Basics of the Heart Chakra

Location	at the center of the chest, between the breasts. As a chakra, it's important to remember that it is multidimensional and sits in the center of the body while emanating energy outward.
Energy	Yang
Element	Air
Mantra	YAM or I love.
Sound	F note, 526 to 606 Hz
Organs	Heart
Spine	T2 to T5
Endocrine System	Thymus Gland
Color	Green

The Main Functions:

The unconditional love heart chakra is driven by the principle of love with complete acceptance. The way we accept a new born child, with love and compassion. This is the love we should have for everyone, accept them for who they are, their strength and their weaknesses.

Love is a transforming energy that transmutes emotions and experiences in the physical body and links it to the Spiritual Heart. It's an essential element of any relationship, it is not just about romance, but about going beyond the limit of the ego and preoccupations with oneself into compassion and acceptance of all that is. A person with an open-heart chakra lives in harmony, is happy, passionate, able to love and be loved, and forgives. Principally oriented towards self-acceptance, and able to balance of female and male energies within oneself.

Unbalanced Chakra

The unbalanced heart creates a lack of connection with others but energetically it also breaks the bridge that links the physical world to the spiritual world. Leading individuals to lead lives based on physical needs, fears and ego needs at the expense of others and one self.

Physical:

Heart palpitations, arrhythmic, heart attack, circulatory disease, blood disorder, blood circulation, high blood pressure.

Etheric:

The memory held by the etheric body are heartbreak and betrayal, it holds on to memory when those we loved judge us and impose condition of loving us. We hold the memories from our life where we have been hurt for trusting others.

Mental:

Can be defensiveness, passive/aggressive behavior, suspiciousness, being judgmental, excessive isolation, recluse, antisocial, discrimination

Emotional:

Tendency to feeling like a victim, being overly defensive, jealousy, fear of intimacy, being codependent by relying on others approval and attention, trying to please at all costs, inability to connect, holding grudges, not being able to forgive, anxious, control, emotional confusion, unloving, uncaring, dysfunctional relationships, grieving.

Spiritual:

Being unable to forgive ourselves.

Healing Your Heart Chakra

To start, you can simply engage in self-care activities, in order to learn to love yourself. You cannot truly love others if we can't love ourselves. It is a time to have a bath, pamper yourself and start accepting all of you just like you accept your best friend. Do you care your best friend has love handles or a double chin or saggy breasts, probably not , so let go of your inner critic and be less judgmental towards oneself? It is important that you understand how you sabotage yourself and work out inner conflicts and find inner peace. Most importantly, you must work on forgiveness.

The color green will help the heart and soul and helps to release emotionally suppressed trauma, wear it on you with clothes or jewelry, add it to your environment with plants or paint. Bath in green colored bath, wear green lens glasses or put in a green lamp shade to emanate the room with green light.

Aroma therapy:

Angelica, bergamot, cedar wood, cloves, cypress, estragon, eucalyptus, galbanum, geranium, hyssop, jasmine, lavender, mandarin, melissa, palmarosa, rose wood, tarragon.

Food:

Vegetables:
Green vegetables like leafy greens, from kale, spinach, chard, collard, dandelion and mustard greens, to lettuce and sprouts of all kinds, and broccoli, Brussel sprouts and cauliflower. There's also Bok choy, cabbage, arugula, green peas and peppers, leeks, green onions, watercress, zucchini, artichoke, asparagus, green peas, kohlrabi and celery.

Fruits:
You should also add green fruit in your diet, from green apples, grapes, honeydew melon, limes, pears and kiwi, to that best salad ingredient of all – avocados.

Rocks & Crystals:

Based on Color:
Amazonite, Chrysocolla, Chrysoprase, Dioptase, Emerald, Green Aventurine, Green Calcite, Green Fluorite, Green Jade, Green Jasper, Green Tourmaline, Malachite, Moldavite, Moss Agate, Peridot, Prehnite.

Frequency:
Apache Tear, Blue Apatite, Blue Opal, Blue Tourmaline, Carnelian, Charoite, Cobalto Calcite, Crocoite, Danburite, Fire Opal, Garnet, Green Apophyllite, Halite, Kunzite, Larimar, Morganite, Pearl, Pink Tourmaline, Rainbow Onyx, Rhodochrosite, Ruby, Shiva Lingam, Stromatolite, Sulfur, Titanium Rainbow Aura Quartz

Yoga:

These positions are intended to broaden the chest area through breath and strengthen the spine:

• Cobra is a great asana for opening the heart chakra
• Bhujangasana
• Cow Face
• Gomukhasana
• Eagle
• Garudasana
• Fish
• Matsyasana
• Cat
• Marjaryasana
• Upward-facing dog
• Urdhva Mukha Svanasana
• Bridge
• Setubandha Sarvangasana
• Wheel
• Urdhva Dhanurasana
• Triangle
• Trikonasana
• Camel
• Ustrasana)

Meditation:

One of my favorite visualizations if I'm feeling a relationship problem, is to imagine a crystal pyramid temple around my heart chakra. The God loving energy entering through the top of the pyramid flooding the heart chakra like a water fall and continuing down towards solar plexus. I imagine the inside of the pyramid filled with greenery and flowers. On the outside, the pyramid is surrounded by grass and shading trees and at the edge of the clearing is the person I'm having difficulty with. Ask yourself if you would like to invite the person in your heart to love and forgive them. If you are not ready to invite the person inside the protective pyramid then surround them with a green glow, send that person love and forgiveness, and through magical thinking, and come back when you are ready to invite them in. Know that you are safe and protected and no one can harm you. There's no need to hide behind walls, castles, or bury ourselves. The crystal is clear, and you choose who you invite in and who you leave out.

For the hand position you may try one of the following:

Shuni Mudra the tips of the middle finger and thumb touch. Place in front of the lower part of your breast bone.
Padma Mudra or Unconditional Love: With fingers pointing upward, bring the heels of the hands together. Keeping the pinky fingers and thumbs together, spread the other fingers. Bring the hands in front of the heart.
Vajrapradama Mudra or self-trust: Interlace fingers from right and left hand to the first knuckle, with the pinky fingers on the bottom. Extend thumbs and index fingers upward. Hold hands in front of the heart and chest with elbows relaxed downward.
Hridaya Mudra or Inner guidance: Place the right hand over the heart. Place the left hand on top of the right hand. Relax the shoulders and lengthen the spine.

The 13th chakra system of ancient Egypt

Ascended Master:

Quan Yin, St-Francis of Assisi.

Archangel:

Archangel Jeremiel and Peace

Kundalini

Kundalini continues to grow and evolve and reach the next level of energy, the energy of love was present through history as we recall the romance and tragic love stories, but it was the gift of the poor. Until recent history, those who were rich, held a title or were landowners would marry to strengthen their position, their wealth. To marry for love was a luxury. Below are some examples of how kundalini can be used for specific themes, such as sexuality, finances, and humanity's growth.

Sexual Kundalini:

Here the sexual energy evolves as an expression of love. Sexuality develops a new meaning, as it transcends its physical nature and becomes a deeper expression of deep feelings where the other person matters as much as we do and through sexuality the energy is exchanged willingly back and forth.

Financial Kundalini:

In matters of resources or money, the love energy makes us think above and beyond our needs into the needs of others.

Humanity's Kundalini:

Humanity does not always grow in leaps and bounds and some areas, countries may arrive at an energy level before another. The old stories of tragic love warned the lovers that to be in love was to tempt faith to a horrible outcome of drama and tragedy. To this day, we are still learning to live without conditions. For so long, a marriage was more about a contract than love and as long as some heirs were provided there was no real obligation to remain faithful. More and more we are finding a higher way to love, without conditions in all its forms.

Chapter 8: Universal Love

When both hearts beat in unison and freely exchange energy then it facilitates integration between the physical and earthly plane needs and spiritual aspirations. It bridges the spiritual and the earthly chakras. When both hearts beat together, they both change to a gold color.

Basics of the Universal Love

Location	It is positioned halfway between the heart and the throat
Energy	**Yin**
Element	**Quantum**
Mantra	LAM (pronounced LANG), or I am.
Sound	F# Note, 800 Hz
Organs	Lungs
Spine	C7 to T1
Endocrine System	The nervous system.
Color	Pink

The Main Functions:

This chakra is about loving without reservation and the ability to share with others without recompense. It governs compassion and to be of service without any expectation in return. This joins your spiritual aspiration with your life goals on the earth. You will make decisions based on awareness and insights. A person with an open and balanced chakra will have empathy, altruism, living in harmony. It connects you to creator, your higher self in fulfilling ways. It allows us to stretch beyond our common sphere of understanding into universal unity with all that is.

Unbalanced Chakra

This chakra is an either open or closed. You are born with it opened however it may close after a burnout or realizing that someone took advantage of our generosity. This is an important life lesson in both cases, as an individual you need to set personal boundaries, you need to learn to say no.

Physical:

Burn out, depression, asthma, allergies, bronchitis, pneumonia, abused chocolate, sugar, early physical aging, chest congestion, hyperventilation, influenza, respiratory problems, shortness of breath, smoking.

Etheric:

This body holds the memory of your soul, your purpose, the reason why you are on earth. To be unbalanced is to go through life without direction and just following the motions. You work but get no joy out of it, you may be a new contributor to society, but you have no passion or joy out of it.

Mental:

You have no boundaries, so you have extended yourself to fulfill other people's perceived needs to the cost of one's own balance, without personal boundaries you are being of service at your own detriment. A person may also be narrow minded.

Emotional:

A person would have a lack of compassion, unable to love, putting themselves ahead and be overly demanding of others. If they are of service, they will require constant acknowledgment and adopt the role of savior or rescuer or be addicted to love

Spiritual:

This is your loss of connection to your purpose. You are rejecting your role because it's a difficult choice or means you will earn less money. You don't feel you are part of the greater universe; you have lost your connection with the soul.

Healing Your Universal Love

To start, you can simply engage in a few hours of volunteering into something you feel comfortable with. A visit to a retirement home, participating in cleaning a park project, helping at school in the classroom or at your local organization. Identify what age group you are most comfortable with and see if they need an extra hand. Just establish how many hours you have to give and stick to it. You need to set boundaries, especially if you have been burned in the past.

You can also wear pink in your clothes, accessories or jewelry. Add a touch of pink in your décor at home or the office.

An effective technique called tapping can be used for the heart, a simple technique used to interact with the thymus gland, tap it lightly with the tip of your fingers, either at the center of the chest at the collar bone level, or on each side about 3 to 4 inches away. The first technique calms the nervous system, the second one tends to bring the level of energy up.

Aroma therapy:

Palmarosa, rose, ylang ylang,

Food:

Vegetables:
Beets, radish, radicchio, red cabbage, red onion, red potato.

Fruit:
Berries, blood orange, cranberries, cherries, pink grapefruit, pink lemonade, pomegranate, red apple, red grapes, rhubarb, strawberry, tomatoes, water melon.

Rocks & Crystals:

Based on Color:

Cobalto calcite, Garnet, Lithium Quartz, Garnet, Pink Opal, Pink Tourmaline, Rhodochrosite, Rhodonite, Rose Aura Quartz, Rose Quartz, Ruby, Spirit Quartz, Watermelon Tourmaline.

The 13th chakra system of ancient Egypt

Frequency:

Aegirine, Anhydrite, Aquamarine, Bloodstone, Blue Topaz, Chrysoberyl, Danburite, Dioptase, Dolomite, Dragon Blood, Emerald, Golden Topaz, Green Calcite, Green fluorite, Howlite, Kunzite, Opal Aura Quartz, Pink Lemurian, Sugilite, Sulfur, Tanzanite, Titanium Rainbow Aura Quartz, Unakite

Yoga:

Same for both hearts.

Meditation:

I enjoy listening to a wonderful singer named Denise Hagan who created an album based on a healthy regular heart beat called, "Numinous". I find this meditation so soothing and calming. You focus on your heartbeat and feel your two hearts beating as one. You feel and hear your hearts beating louder and steadier in your chest. Be united in your hearts so the physical and spiritual work together towards a soul filled life in all aspect of your life.

You have 3 Mudra choices to accompany your meditation:

Bhramara Mudra or Breath : Bring the tip of the index fingers to touch the base of the thumbs. Touch the tip of the thumbs to the top of the middle finger. Allow all other fingers to extend outward. Rest the backs of the hands on the tops of the thighs, palm facing up.
Uttarabodhi Mudra or Awakening: Interlace the fingers of both hands with the tips of the thumbs touching and pointing downward. Extend the index fingers upward, touching them together. Bring the hands close to the heart center.
Tejas Mudra or Brilliance: Bend the two index fingers, softly touching them together. Bring the thumbs together facing upward. Spread the other fingers apart and wide. Hold the mudra in front of the heart a few inches away from the body.

Ascended Master:

Ascended Master Paul the Venetian for love, charity and beauty and Maha Chohan.

Archangel:

Archangel Chamuel and Charity.

Kundalini:

As the energy of the two hearts mixes and works to unite the kundalini to rise into universal love, a love above all else, the love of our divine creator, the love from our higher self. A pure connection, that reminds us we are never alone and never without love.

Financial Kundalini:

This energy helps people come together and raise awareness of others who need help. This can take the form of raising money for causes or help for areas devastated by earthquakes or tsunamis. Any organization that works towards raising money to help fund hospitals, research or to grant a wish for terminally ill patients.

Humanity's Kundalini:

Humanity has had great examples of people living in their universal love energy such as Jesus, Ghandi, Mandela and Mother Theresa. They dedicated their life into service for the greater good without ever expecting anything in return. There are more and more examples of people who are changing others, nature or animal life by giving their time, sharing their food or taking on responsibilities that are not theirs because they know something is wrong and it requires change and decide to be that change. They are an example and an inspiration to follow, we can't all be a full-time giver like Mother Theresa was, but we can make a huge difference even a few hours a week. There are over 7 billion people on the planet, if everyone was giving a few hours a week to a cause to help others be in a better, healthier safer place, in a short time we would overcome poverty, famine and sickness. There is no lack of food or money, it just needs to be distributed more evenly.

Chapter 9: Hands Chakra

The hands channel energy from the throat chakra and universal love chakra therefore the hands are a means of communication, either through actual sign language, by helping others or by exchanging energy. It is through the hands that most energy healing is channeled.

Basics of the hand Chakra

Location	The entire hands or focused with the palm of the hand or manipulated through the finger tips
Energy	**Yang** right hand, **Yin** left hand.
Element	**Fire**
Mantra	HUM or I help.
Sound	F# Note, 565 Hz
Organs	the hands, arms, shoulder
Spine	It encompasses the first three vertebrae at the pelvic plexus.
Endocrine System	Immune system.
Color	Deep purple.

The Main Functions: Healing purpose.

The hands are not considered a main chakra, yet in the Egyptian culture, they are a main center to transmit the energy, move energy, transfer energy and were once recognized as an important exchange center and in this book the hands are given a proper place in their role in self-healing, healing others and Mother Nature. To help others we must first make sure we are balanced, it's important to be empowered. As healers go through life, they also need time to heal themselves. It is important to recognize when you are in a situation of crisis and/or unbalanced to take some time for themselves to heal before they start trying to heal others.

Unbalanced Chakra

The unbalanced chakra would present a multitude of symptoms in the different bodies. The hands are being used every day in everything we do, we touch, we prepare our food, eat, we feel through our hands. Blocked chakras are the inability to care for ourselves, or those in our charge.

Physical:

Arthritis, shoulder pain, tennis elbow, carpal tunnel syndrome, tendonitis, cyst, tendon, chronic epicondylitis, isolation wart, perspiration.

Etheric:

The memory held in a blocked chakra is represented by old ideas, values, traditions and thoughts that no longer serve you or were never yours to start with but that you continue to use even though it's not your truth.

Mental:

As the hand chakra is fed by energy from the universal heart and the throat, we see similar mental afflictions like a burn-out, compares himself/herself to others and is very competitive as opposed to being helpful. Unable to receive unconditionally, feeling guilty.

Spiritual:

The person often feels ungrounded, spacey, and lost in thoughts and unable to heal.

Emotional:

A person would seek isolation, may suffer from phobias of germs or contact. The person who has suffered a burn out may feel undervalued and frustrated, anxious and/or anger, be unable to ask for help.

Healing the hand chakra

The hands are our tools to link ourselves to the outside world. We use our hands for everything from caring for our bodies, cooking our food, eating our food, and nurturing others. If our hands or arms are crippled or ineffective it affects us on some deep level and affects our independence to support ourselves. Our inability to care for ourselves eventually cripples us and makes us dependent on others. The hands help us enhance our creativity. The methods vary a little for the hands, since our hands are the base of any care, we need to now care for ourselves and open up to others. To start, you can simply wash your hands and apply hand cream, wear gloves, give yourself a manicure, care for your hands. Try simple crafts, such as coloring, knitting or crochet, massage your hands. Eat your food with your hands.

Aroma therapy:

Carrot seed, frankincense, German chamomile, geranium, helichrysum, lavender, myrrh, neroli, palmarosa, rosemary, rose, roman chamomile, sandalwood. *For arthritis:* citrus, jasmine, peppermint.

Food:

Kale, broccoli, spinach and especially high-antioxidant foods loaded with vitamin C, vitamin K and minerals that speed up the healing process. Another benefit of these foods is that most are packed in zinc (pumpkin seeds and spinach) and berries.

Rocks & Crystals:

Based on Color: Diamond, Herkimer Diamond, Lemurian, Opalite, Pearls, Quartz.

Frequency :

Blue Kyanite, Blue Sapphire, Blue Topaz, Clear Apophyllite, Golden Healer Quartz, Green Apophyllite, Green Jasper, Pink Lemurian, Prehnite, Snowflake Obsidian, Sulfur, Titanium Rainbow Aura Quartz, Unakite.

Yoga:

This is where the Mudras (hand position) come into play. There are several ways to join the fingers or position the hand in order to move energy.

I would also recommend a tai chi practice. Most yoga positions require strong and flexible hands to accomplish any position as opposed to Tai chi that helps you regain movement, flexibility and requires no actual strength. Tai chi helps you manipulate energy and return gracefulness to your hands.

Meditation:

Try growing a ball of light between your hands and then see the energy bouncing from one hand to another. You can then spread the energy like cream over your hands and repeat.

Ascended Master:

Ascended master Melchisedek.

Archangel:

Sandalphon and Archangel Shekhinakà

Kundalini

Through our hands we create, we share, we make contact. Below are some examples of how kundalini can be used for specific themes, such as sexuality, finances, and humanity's growth.

Sexual Kundalini:

The sexual energy transmitted to the hands allows for the energy to be transmitted by touch, massage, the contact of skin can spark partners with grace, subtle movement. The discreet touch of lovers trying to escape their chaperon.

Financial Kundalini:

The hands play a great role in the exchange of money, of barter. The energy of the hands in financial matters evolves to a fair and balanced exchange. A proper compensation for services received or goods offered.

Humanity's Kundalini:

We are in a time where energy healers are more and more available. There are several forms of energy healing from Reiki, healing hands, body talk, psych-K all work towards moving and directing energy for healing, balancing and restoring a person to good health. This ability to heal with the hands is not new, it was popular among shaman in aboriginal tribes. It is also through hands that the traditional medicine took its course, it is through the hands and touch that patients received their care.

Chapter 10: Throat Chakra

The Throat chakra is the center of communication. It expends from the throat, the inner and outer ears, mouth, tongue, teeth because communication is as much as sharing our truth, our message as it is to listen to others, their ideas and perspective without fears. We communicate verbally, non-verbally through sighs, eye rolls or be writing. The throat chakra encompasses all means of communication, sharing, understanding in respect and in truth.

Basics of the Throat Chakra

Location	at the level of the throat, the mouth and ears.
Energy	**Yin**
Element	**Ether**
Mantra	HAM or I speak
Sound	G note, 606 to 670 HZ
Organs	Bronchial tubes, vocal cords, all areas of the mouth, jaws, tongue, pharynx and palate, the shoulders and the neck.
Spine	C3 to C6
Endocrine System	Thyroid and parathyroid gland, they regulate the body temperature and metabolism.
Color	Light blue

The Main Functions:

The Throat chakra is your ability to communicate, listen, verbalize and express our needs, emotional independence, it is the gate to truthful existence. A balanced throat chakra enables fearless truthful expression and empathetic listening, without ever harming others with our speech. The emphasis is on expressing and projecting the creativity into the world, being authentic and the ability to speak our highest truth. It is also a way express our creativity through sound, vibration and singing.

Unbalanced Chakra

A person will use their voice in a vulgar, sarcastic way, with anger. They will not be able to communicate their feelings, or thoughts in a rational manner and are unable to speak their truth.

Physical:

A person might feel hoarseness, sore throat, thyroid issues, laryngitis, neck pain, ear aches, frequent headaches, dental issues, mouth ulcers, temporomandibular disorders of the jaw (known as TMJ). A person may lack of control over one's speech, include gossiping, non-stop talking or have a small and imperceptible voice, compulsive or excessive eating, hearing problems, hoarseness, laryngitis, lost voice, mouth ulcer, sore throat, stammer, stiff neck, teeth/gums, tinnitus, tonsils, whooping cough.

Etheric:

The memory of your ability to express yourself is contained here and speaking your truth might have been affected by trauma, abuse or threats. Recovering your ability to speak your truth requires you to face your fears of being mocked or your fear of freezing.

Mental:

Your ability to speak first emanates from your thoughts, someone with a blocked chakra will have incessant mental discourse, your thoughts going around in circles being unable to form a proper sentence or you can't formulate what you are trying to express, bringing a sense of confusion, a person may display arrogance, use condescension or be manipulative. They will suffer social anxiety, inhibited creativity, stubbornness, depression, aggression, lack of self-esteem.

Emotional:

A person who cannot express themselves suffers from insecurity, timidity, introversion, excessive fear of speaking or will be found compensating their inability to speak their truth by gossiping, nonstop talking and being verbally aggressive or mean. They are also unable to listen to others, have inconsistency in their speech and actions, demonstrating detachment.

Spiritual:

The person will have lost their voice, they will have lost their ability to express their truth and be lost in their ability to express their spirituality and their faith without fear of persecution. They will hide their identity from the outside world because they fear the world's reaction and rejection.

Healing Your Throat Chakra

To start, you can simply start incorporating the color blue into your decor at home and work. Another subtle way to balance your chakra is to wear blue clothes, accessories or jewelry. **"Tea it out"**, talk openly with close friends or a family member that is a nurturer for you. Make it a point to be open and honest with all you say. Simply speaking in a heartfelt way can work wonders to strengthen and balance the throat chakra. Learning how to express yourself without censoring or editing can be valuable. Practice journaling explore your ideas, your emotions and keep track of your progress. Try your hand at poetry, lyrics or short stories. Let creativity help you express how you feel, what you have been burying for so long.

"Let It go", whatever you are holding is preventing you from moving forward, let go of all things you have no control over. Let go of resentment, guilt, and anger.

Aroma therapy:

Allspice, basil, bergamot, calendula, camphor, chamomile, coriander, cypress, eucalyptus, geranium, jasmine, lavender, peppermint, petitgrain, rosemary, sandalwood, spearmint, tuberose, ylang-ylang.

Food:

Vegetables:
Eggplant, purple asparagus, purple cabbage, purple carrots, purple peppers, purple potatoes and purple kohlrabi.

Fruit:
Apples, blackberries, black currants, blueberries, elderberries, honey, lemon, limes figs, peaches, plums, prunes, raisins, purple grapes.

Rocks & Crystals:

Based on Color:
Amazonite, Angelite, Aqua Aura quartz, Aquamarine, Azurite, Blue Calcite, Blue Fluorite, Blue Kyanite, Blue Lace Agate, Blue Quartz, Blue Sapphire, Blue Topaz, Blue Tourmaline, Cavansite, Dumortierite, Hemimorphite, Lapis Lazuli, Sodalite, Tanzanite, Tanzanite Aura Quartz, Turquoise.

Frequency:
Blue Apatite, Chrysocolla, Cobalto Calcite, Dragon Blood, Larimar, Milky Quartz, Moldavite, Opalite, Rose Aura Quartz, Sulfur Titanium Rainbow Aura Quartz, Tourmalinated Quartz, Yellow Mookaite

Yoga:

These poses will help you open your throat chakra:

• Camel • Ustrasana
• Plow • Halasana
• Bridge • Setu Bandha Sarvangasana
• Fish • Matsyasana
• Standing forward bend • Uttanasana
• Shoulder stand • Salamba Sarvangasana
• The wheel • upward bow • hakrasana
• Side angle pose • Utthita Parsvakonasana

Meditation:

"Sing", singing can help dispel blockages, activate, and balance. If you doubt your ability to sing, start with toning the mantra for the throat chakra and move to other chakra mantras, humming is also an option. Get used to listening to your voice while you are in your sacred space.

For the hand position:

Dyana Mudra, just cross fingers on the inside of hands. Let thumbs touch at the tops, pull slightly up.
Garuda Mudra or Freedom: Bring the left hand in front of the heart, palm facing in and thumb facing upward. Cross the back of the right hand behind the left palm until the thumbs meet. Interlace the thumbs and fan the rest of the fingers outward. Bring the mudra up to the throat center
Samputa Mudra or Inner truth: Hold left hand cupped facing upward. Bring right hand, palm facing down, cupped over the top of left hand with fingers resting on the outer edge of left thumb. Bring hands into the belly center.

.

Ascended Master:

El Morya

Archangel:

Archangels Gabriel, Michael and Faith.

Kundalini

Through our throat we communicate and listen. When our kundalini raises to our throat we speak with love, forgiveness, peaceful and calm words.

Sexual Kundalini:

This is where the connection takes the form of expression, through language, touch and non-spoken. It is a place where each partner can express their truth and be respected and honored in their body, their emotions and their mind.

Financial Kundalini:

The energy moves from a form of sharing of resources by communicating what is available and establishing an exchange.

Humanity's Kundalini:

Humanity has reached breakthroughs that are comparatively immeasurable to the past thousands of years. Going at first, from oral traditions to some cultures with a written form that held records. Communication did not evolve much, the ability to read and write was limited to the few who viewed this ability as a privilege and not a right. It's only just recently that basic education has been offered to a larger population and not even world-wide yet. However, with the invention of the telegraph, telephones, and more recently internet allowing us to see and do a live chat has created great possibilities to communicate in real time all over the world. This resurgence of electronic communication can be associated to the reincarnation of the Atlantean souls in the human evolution.

Chapter 11: Manifesting center

The Manifestation center or the center of thoughts comes from the Egyptian system. It is an important energy center that focuses the energy of our thoughts into creating our world. This is where your co-creating ability stems from. Your thoughts are undoubtably your first action. If you decide to put more energy into your thoughts, they become actions in the third dimension. Your thoughts are powerful and hold a strong vibrational capability. They affect not just your head but your entire Universe.

Basics of the Manifestation Chakra

Location	It sits between the throat and the 3rd eye at the center of the head behind the nose.
Energy	Yang
Element	Ether
Mantra	HRIM or I think
Sound	G# note, 900Hz
Organs	Brain
Spine	C2
Endocrine System	The pituitary gland and works in partnership with the pineal gland for balance.
Color	Moon light silver, it is characterized by the quality of its luminescence or soft radiance that reminds us of the moon light and or Aqua.

The Main Functions:

It emphasizes the mind as a powerful tool to shape matter. Your thoughts are your tool to co-create. Each of your thoughts is powered up by a healthy chakra to manifest what you need to achieve your soul's purpose. It is associated with the energies of the moon. It is the center of intelligence, thinking, imagination, awareness and ideas

Unbalanced Chakra
The chakra that is blocked renders a person unable to know what they need, their thoughts are like a storm inside their head, they are confused and unable to stick to a decision or follow through.

Physical:

This manifests as headaches, migraines, mental confusion, chronic tiredness, brain tumors, growth issues, nervous breakdowns.

Etheric:

The memory held in this chakra has to do with your ability to manifest and be a co-creator. It is your inability to remember that this third dimension is just a play on a large-scale stage. This is the illusion and all life, objects and things are made of energy and we can control and manipulate this energy to create what we need.

Mental:

The thoughts are confused, mixed up and unstable. It's a loss of focus, ADHD and ADD, paranoia are prime examples of a blocked chakra.

Emotional:

It is the seat of many mental illnesses like depression, PTSD, bipolar disorder, OCD. It is the disease of the mind poisoned and unable to forget abuse or trauma that is stuck in a repetition of the nightmare without an exit.

Spiritual:

A person having lost touch with their mind, their ability to think rationally is lost and unable to make decisions to alter their path. They feel hopelessness and helplessness up to the point that it can lead to suicide.

Healing Your Manifestation Chakra

To start, if you suspect that you suffer from a mental illness, you should see your doctor, modern medicine can certainly help restore the chemical imbalance of the brain to get you out of the tormented storm. There is nothing wrong with seeking help from a medical professional. Herbs have been used for centuries to help with those disorders and are a much-needed support to re-ascend into the light. Behavioral therapy and re-education are also very important in making new brain connections to heal from a brain trauma or to create new pathways that circumvent the area affected by situational memory issues. I do believe you can heal your mind, create new pathways. There is now a technology that lets you watch a screen while your brain waves are monitored and readjust your brain waves when they fall below normal range with a flash of light. It's non-invasive and relatively quick. There are many ways to re-educate the brain to produce the chemical required for the connections to take place. This is a field that has made huge progress in the last century.

You can help your healing curve by supplementing your therapy with the following methods as well. However, if your depression or symptoms are severe, I do recommend you see a doctor, naturopath or other health professional to have support and help on your journey back to health.

Aroma therapy:

Arborvitae, basil, clary sage, cypress, lavender, lemon, lemongrass, geranium, peppermint, rosemary, ylang-ylang.

Food:

Vegetables:
Artichoke, cauliflower, chives, fennel, garlic, ginger, green onion, Jerusalem, jicama, kohlrabi, leeks, mushrooms, onions, parsnips, potatoes and shallots.

Fruit:
Bananas, white pears, white nectarines.

Rocks & Crystals:

Color: Aqua Aura Quartz, Blue Topaz, Milky Quartz, Opal, Pearl Sardonyx

Frequency:

Aegirine, Amazonite, Amber, Aquamarine, Auralite 23, Beryl, Black Jasper, Black Obsidian, Blue Apatite, Blue Onyx, Blue Quartz, Blue Sapphire, Cavansite, Chiastolite, Chrysoberyl, Cinnabrite, Cobalto Calcite, Citrine, Covellite, Danburite, Desert Rose, Diamond, Dioptase, Dumortierite, Emerald, Gold Quartz, Golden Calcite, Golden Danburite, Golden Fluorite, Golden Topaz, Green Calcite, Grey Jasper, Heliodor, Hematite, Hessonite, Howlite, Lazulite, Lemurian Jade, Lepidolite, Lodolite, Malachite, Meteorite, Moonstone, Mount Shasta Serpentine, Nuummite, Peridot, Pink Lemurian, Preseli Bluestone, Pyrite, Rainbow Fluorite, Rainbow Moonstone, Rainbow Onyx, Red Aventurine, Rutile, Schalenblende, Septarian, Smokey Quartz, Sodalite, Staurolite, Stilbite, Stibnite, Sulfur, Tangerine Quartz, Tanzanite, Tibetan Quartz, Tiger Eye, Titanium Rainbow Aura Quartz, Trolleite, Violet Flame Opal, Yellow Jasper rainbow moonstone, selenite

Yoga:

For specific yoga positions, I recommend you complete the throat and 3rd eye exercises. I also encourage you to get an acupuncture treatment and a chiropractic adjustment. Those two-ancient methods of healing can help the limbic and lymphatic system to work and for the skeletal frame to be straight and stop the strain on the muscles and nerves.

Meditation:

This is the hardest chakra to meditate with since your mind won't stop, your thoughts won't quiet down. As you try, close your eyes, and try to visualize a simple image of a flame or flower, see what thoughts come to mind and write them down. Let thoughts come, whether it is about buying milk, to gassing up the car or the fact that you still have laundry to do, just write it down. Your mind is in overdrive and you need to release your worries out of your mind. Your mind will be able to let go if it knows you won't forget. After your mediation is complete, then make a list and organize what you need to do in an efficient way to save time and money. Buy an agenda to keep track of all your appointments, obligations and write down your to do list giving yourself enough time to complete the tasks. Free your head of daily tasks and leave the third dimension to spend more time during your meditation in your spiritual body. The hand position will help you clean your thoughts and old thought forms, you may choose amongst the following:

Vishuddha Mudra or Purification: Bring the tips of the thumbs to touch the base of the ring fingers and curl them up. Allow all other fingers to extend outward away from the body. Rest the backs of the hands on the tops of the thighs.

Kali Mudra or Release: Interlace the fingers of both hands in front of the heart with the right thumb over the left. Extend the index fingers upward toward the throat center.

Trishula Mudra or Unity: Bend the pinky fingers inward to rest on the base of the thumb. Lay the thumbs over the pinky fingers. Extend other fingers straight out. Hold the hands away from the body, fingers facing outward.

Ascended Master:

White Buffalo woman.

Archangel:

Archangel Ariel and Courage

Kundalini

Through our manifestation center, we create from thoughts, we use the quantum energy and give it to our ideas and thoughts and create our reality. All thoughts are created equal and have the potential to create something good or something bad. Even if the thought is never put into words or action, it is given life energetically. This affects your personal energy. The more focused your thoughts are in fantasies or violent, the more you breed the energy in your own field. Below are some examples of how kundalini can be used for specific themes, such as sexuality, finances, and humanity's growth.

Sexual Kundalini:

The sexual energy can be used to create and manifest a loving, caring relationship. A kundalini that is obstructed by fantasy can negatively affect a person's ability to create a balanced, loving relationship.

Financial Kundalini:

The key to manifestation is based not on ego but on Soul's purpose. The awakened kundalini will power up the energy required to create and manifest the resources or money required to help the soul move forward on its soul path. If you are not getting what you want, you must ask yourself why you are not manifesting what you need. Is it because you confused your needs with what your ego wants? A healthy Kundalini is a kundalini that works for the betterment of the world not just our personal life. As our efforts benefit the world, they automatically benefit us.

Humanity's Kundalini:

We are in a time where people like Louise Hay who has spent time trying to teach people about affirmations. It is a time where Kryon teaches us to word it out, our wishes and ground them into making this world a better place and say it out loud or Bruce Lipton in his book "Biology of beliefs" which talks about discovering the power of the mind to learn how to create a healthy and harmonious life experience. Without forgetting, Rob Williams who developed PSYCH-K®. A method that allows you to quickly and painlessly change the subconscious beliefs that limit the full expression of your potential in life, as a spiritual being.

The 13th chakra system of ancient Egypt

Manifesting is fairly new in our history and we must become completely aware of the power of our thoughts and be careful of what we think about. Our thoughts are influenced by our daily lives. What are you reading? What are you listening to? What kind of television shows do you watch? All those things are affecting your thoughts, and consequently our lives. Be mindful of what you feed your brain. This is still at a stage of evolution and many of us still require time to learn and put into practice our abilities to manifest not for the ego but for the good of our community and the world. Children are our best teachers, the way the internet as helped them grow and become aware of world issues and they work at raising money, building wells and helping those less fortunate than them. They are a shining example of what we are all capable of once we stop hoarding and distribute the resources equally.

Chapter 12: 3rd eye Chakra

The pituitary gland produces hormones and governs the function of the previous five glands; sometimes, the pineal gland is linked to the third eye chakra as well as to the crown chakra. the pineal gland is in charge of regulating biorhythms, including sleep and wake time. It's a gland located in the brain that is a center of attention because of its relationship with the perception and effect of light and altered or "mystical" states of consciousness

This is where all the extra sensory perception gifts connect to, Clairvoyance, Clairsentience, and Clair gnostic. The seat of inspiration that helps you visualize and implement creative ideas. This is the place where you can get guidance for the bigger picture and connecting to your higher self. This is where we access a mystical state and achieve illumination from the divine.

Basics of the 3rd eye Chakra

Location	It is located in the middle of the forehead between the brows
Energy	Yang
Element	Etheric
Mantra	Ksham, or I see
Sound	A note, 632 to 852 Hz
Organs	Eyes
Spine	C1
Endocrine System	The pituitary gland; the pineal gland
Color	Indigo, it helps us see perfection in all things

The Main Functions:

This is the center of intuition, understanding, for gifts to get past the veil of the third dimension, guiding dreams, and mediumship. This helps you receive guidance in your everyday life and access to all your senses. This helps you realize you are not alone and helps your thoughts to become reality through vision. A healthy and strong 3rd eye chakra lets the individual be fearless, and have the ability to focus, meditate, visualize.

It is our center of intuition. This center is where imagination grows and helps you get in touch with universal wisdom.

Unbalanced Chakra
A person may experience feeling stuck in the daily grind without being able to look beyond your problems and set a guiding vision for yourself.

Physical:

May include headaches, vision problems, seizures, insomnia, nausea, sinus issues, amnesia, anxiety, blindness, brain tumor, cataracts, dizziness, dyslexia, fainting spells, glaucoma, tremors.

Etheric:

The body remembers the higher-self body, and it remembers scars, old injuries and lost limbs and phantom pains.

Mental:

They can be hallucinations, being judgmental, mental fog, and/or delusions. In less blocked chakra, one can feel they have no sense of logic.

Emotional:

Anxiety, feeling overwhelmed, paranoia, depressive, remote, undisciplined, a person who suffers from intolerance and has no empathy.

Spiritual:

Indulgence in psychic fantasies and illusions that appear more real than reality, a lack of clarity or inability to see the bigger picture that robs us from being able to establish a vision for oneself and realize it, rejection of everything spiritual or beyond the usual.

Healing Your 3rd eye Chakra

Stimulate your intuitive side, this will help you receive guidance and trust yourself more. Explore your mystical and mysterious side and try to explore your ability. You could be clairvoyant which is the ability to see beyond the veil and the 3rd dimensional world. You can see Aura colors, spirit guides, and energy around plants or animals. You could be clairaudient which means you are able to hear messages, even a ringing in your ear means that spirit is trying to talk to you.

You could be clairsentient which is your ability to feel others, so many people can actually do this without knowing it. You can collect other people's feelings or energy especially when you are in a public space. If you get tired quickly in public or suffer headaches and migraines after being out in public, you are most likely a clairsentient person. You could also have claircognizance which means you ask yourself a question and automatically know the answer without really knowing where it comes from. Lastly, there are two more senses that can be used to sense energy, or the presence of angels or illness and they are clairgustance which allows you to taste and clairalience that allows you to smell.

Aroma therapy:

Angelica root, bay laurel, basil, bergamot, clary sage, cypress, elemi, frankincense, geranium, juniper, lavender, lemon, lemongrass, marjoram, orange, patchouli, peppermint, rosemary, vanilla, violet, ylang-ylang.

Food:

Purple kohlrabi, purple cabbage, purple carrots, elderberries, figs, purple grapes, purple asparagus

Rocks & Crystals:

Based on Color:
Amethyst, Blue Lace Agate, Blue Sapphire, Blue Tourmaline, Cavansite, Celestite, Chevron Amethyst, Dumortierite, Iolite, Lapis Lazuli, Lithium Quartz, Mystic Topaz, Purple Fluorite, Sodalite, Super Seven, Tanzanite, Tanzanite Aura Quartz, Trolleite, Violet Flame Opal

The 13th chakra system of ancient Egypt

Frequency:
Ametrine, Angel Phantom Quartz, Angelite, Atlantisite, Azurite, Black Jasper, Black Obsidian, Black Onyx, Bloodstone, Blue Apatite, Blue Kyanite, Blue Onyx, Blue Opal, Charoite, Chiastolite, Chlorite Phantom, Chrysocolla, Cinnabrite, Clear Apophyllite, Cobalto Calcite, Covellite, Danburite, Desert Rose, Diamond, Galaxyite, Golden Calcite, Golden Danburite, Golden Topaz, Grape Agate Green Apophyllite, Hemimorphite, Herkimer Diamond, Hessonite, Infinite, Labradorite, Larimar, Lazulite, Lemurian, Lepidolite, Lodolite, Milky Quartz, Moldavite, Moonstone, Mystic Merlinite, Nirvana Quartz, Opalite, Pearl, Peridot, Petalite, Picasso Marble, Pietersite, Pink Opal, Prehnite, Preseli Bluestone, Rainbow Fluorite, Red Jasper, Rhodochrosite, Rhodonite, Ruby, Rutile, Scolecite, Selenite, Serpentine, Shaman Stone, Shiva Eye, Singing Lemurian, Smokey quartz, Staurolite, Stromatolite, Stilbite, Stibnite , Sugilite, Sulfur, Tangerine Quartz, Tangerine Aura Quartz, Tiger Eye, Tiger Iron, Titanium Rainbow Aura Quartz, Tourmalinated Quartz, Turquoise, Vanadinite, White Calcite

Yoga:

• Downward-facing dog • Adho Mukha Svanasana
• Child's pose • Balasana
• Supported shoulder stand • Salamba Sarvangasana
• Big toe • Padangusthasana
• Hero • Virasana
• Head to knee pose • Janu Sirsasana
• Dolphin pose • Makarasana
• Lotus • Sukasana
• Plank • Phalakasana
• Warrior 3 • Virabhadrasana III
• Eagle pose • Garudasana
• Peacock pose • Mayurasana
• Head to knee wide angle pose • Janu Sirsasana
• Standing half forward bend • Ardha Uttanasana

Meditation:

Trataka or Candle Gazing: You may want to practice looking at a flame and closing your eyes and trying to picture a flame. If you lose the image, then open your eyes and look at the flame again. Once you are able to retain the flame image continue on mediating with colored balls of red, orange, yellow, green, pink, blue, aqua, indigo, purple, violet. This will help you meditate on your chakras and seeing them in healthy state. While you meditate, you can ask yourself a question and receive the answer with images or words.Choose amongst one of the following mudras to complete your meditation:

Kalesvara Mudra: bring the tips of your middle finger together pointing up straight. bring the first and middle joint of the index finger together. Thumbs touch and point towards you and down. Creating a heart shape, gently curl the remaining fingers in and connect thumbs to the sternum.
Sakshi Mudra or Inner Witness: Join the tips of all fingers together pointing upward, base of the palms together. Soften the knuckles away from each other. Align the thumbs and bend from the tip to the knuckle facing inward.
Dhyana Mudra or Contemplation: Lay the back of the right hand onto the fingers of the left hand. Bend the index fingers and align them at the first and second joints. Lightly touch the tips of both index fingers to the tops of the thumbs.
Jnana Mudra or Higher knowledge: Touch the tip of the index finger to the tip of the thumb forming a circle. All other fingers extend outward. Rest the backs of the palms on the tops of the thighs, palms facing upward.
Citta Mudra or Consciousness: Bring the palms of the hands together, touching the pads of all the fingers together. Align the thumbs, nails facing outward. Bend the index finger outward with the tips of the fingers touching and connect with the tops of the thumbs.

The 13th chakra system of ancient Egypt

Ascended Master:

Ascended Master Hilarion for truth, vision and prosperity;

Archangel:

Archangel Raphaël and Mother Mary.

Kundalini

Through our 3rd eye chakra, we connect and receive guidance from our highest good. Below are some examples of how kundalini can be used for specific themes, such as sexuality, finances, and humanity's growth.

Sexual Kundalini:

The sexual energy transmitted through the third eye allows two persons to unite outside of time and space. It is possible to unite the energy and reach a new level of closeness and consciousness that unites the two souls and allows them to communicate and reach into their past life. It also allows one to connect with their many incarnations.

Financial Kundalini:

The third eye offers an ability to tap into your intuition and help you plan your path using your resources in the most effective way. Recognizing how to best use what is at your disposal in order to embrace your higher path and your soul's purpose.

Humanity's Kundalini:

Humanity is still struggling in piercing through the veil and understanding that living on earth is just an experiment and a place to learn and evolve in order to return to our spirit form evolved and perfect. Certain individuals are able to see past the veil and they have tried to teach us, help us learn like Jesus and Buddha. However, more and more people are starting to open up to their gift and abilities. The world is opening to the idea that there is more to life than just being born, living and dying. The inequality will soon be a thing of the past once people realize that nothing of this world truly matters because this life is just a play on a grand scale theater. Everything is made of energy, once we truly master our third eye's ability to its full potential, we will manifest out of the air what we need. We will no longer hunger since we will feed from Prana, life giving energy.

Chapter 13: Crown Chakra

It is our connection to the greater world beyond, outside of time and space. When opened, this chakra brings us knowledge, wisdom, understanding, spiritual connection, and bliss. It allows you to connect with your higher self, your true nature as a part of the universe and achieve transcendence. It overcomes your 3rd dimensional preoccupation and helps you see the bigger picture and align yourself with your soul purpose. An open Crown chakra helps you align yourself with helpers and grow your awareness of your goals into a higher consciousness. It allows you to see with clarity and make choices that keep you on track.

Basics of the Crown Chakra

Location	It is located at the top of the head; it radiates upward and is often represented as a ball inside of a lotus with 1000 petals.
Energy	Yin
Element	Etheric
Mantra	Ohm or I know
Sound	B note, 1100 to 1200 Hz
Organs	Spinal cord and brain stem
Spine	Cranium
Endocrine System	Pineal gland and the hypothalamus. The hypothalamus and pituitary gland work in pairs to regulate the endocrine system. The crown chakra is also associated with the brain and the whole nervous system.
Color	Violet, it is also possible that it may be represented by the color white, deep purple, gold or clear.

The Main Functions:

With this chakra, we enter realms transcending space and time. This energy center is said to open access to parallel universes and lives; it gives access to the realm of the Akashic records and the sphere of potentialities in the making. It is a useful center for shamanic healing and communication with spirit guides.

Unbalanced Chakra

An unbalanced Crown chakra means you are disconnected from spirit. A person will express constant cynicism and close mindedness or obsessed with spiritual matters or feeling disconnected spiritually. It can also be represented by a disconnection of the body, living in your head. It also means the person is incapable of setting or maintaining goals, lack of direction.

Physical:

Symptoms include neurological disorders, pineal gland disorder, Alzheimer's, amnesia, epilepsy, immune system, learning difficulties, multiple sclerosis, multiple personality syndrome, neurosis, paralysis, Parkinson's disease, recurring headaches, migraines, schizophrenia and delusional disorders. It also presents itself as insomnia, depression, tiredness, tremors and vomiting.

Etheric:

The memory of old limiting patterns are held here.

Mental:

The symptoms may include depression, a lack of empathy, dizziness, confusion, mental fogginess, seizures or light sensitivity, psychosis, schizophrenia, senile dementia.

Emotional:

This develops into an inability to connect to others.

Spiritual:

This takes the form of areligious, atheist or agnostic.

Healing Your Crown Chakra

It will help you be in control of your emotions, use your intuition effectively and be connected to the divine. To start, you can simply engage in clearing your thoughts and developing your connection to your higher power. If you are an atheist, I encourage you to reconcile what prevents you from believing in a higher power. An open and healed chakra requires that you recognize that there is something greater than you. An energy or a being that represents a divine energy that is with you at all times. There is no other way to have an open crown chakra.

Aroma therapy:

Benzoin, calming blend, cardamom, cedarwood, clary sage, clove, elemi, eucalyptus, frankincense, galbanum, gurjum, helichrysum, jasmine, lavender, myrrh, myrtle, neroli, patchouli, peppermint, rose, rosemary, rosewood.

Food:

Blackberries, black currants, black radish, plums, prunes, purple pepper, purple potatoes, raisins, red onion.

It is always preferable to eat pure food, non-modified, organically grown to help keep your vibration high.

Rocks & Crystals:

Based on Color:
Amethyst, Auralite 23, Charoite, Chevron Amethyst, Galaxyite, Grape Agate, Lepidolite, Nirvana Quartz, Purple Fluorite, Spirit quartz, Scolecite, Sugilite, Super Seven, Tanzanite, Tourmalinated Quartz, Violet Flame Opal

Frequency:
Ametrine, Angel Phantom Quartz, Angelite, Aqua Aura Quartz, Azurite, Black Kyanite, Black Sapphire, Black Tourmaline, Blue Calcite, Blue Fluorite, Blue Kyanite, Blue Opal, Blue Sapphire, Blue Topaz, Chiastolite, Cinnabrite, Clear Apophyllite, Cobalto Calcite, Danburite, Diamond, Dioptase, Dolomite, Dumortierite, Epidote, Fairy Stone, Golden Calcite, Golden Topaz, Green Jasper, Halite, Hemimorphite, Herkimer Diamond, Howlite, Infinite, Kunzite, Labradorite, Lapis

Lazuli, Larimar, Lazulite, Lemurian, Lemurian Jade, Malachite, Mystic Merlinite, Nephrite Jade, Pink Lemurian, Pink Opal, Pietersite, Preseli Bluestone, Pyrite, Quartz, Rainbow Moonstone, Red Tiger Eye, Rutilated Quartz, Schalenblende, Serpentine, Shaman Stone, Shiva Lingam, Singing Lemurian Sodalite, Stilbite, Stibnite, Sulfur, Tibetan Quartz, Titanium Rainbow Aura Quartz, Trolleite, Turquoise, Unakite, Watermelon Tourmaline, White Calcite

Yoga:

• Supported shoulder stand • Salamba Sarvangasana
• Lotus • Padmasana
• Plow • Halasana
• Supported headstand • Salamba Sirsasana
• Reclining bound angle • Supta Baddha Konasana
• Dancer pose. • Natarajasana
• Seated forward bend • Paschimottanasana

Meditation:

This is a meditation that is best practiced as a journey, with a rhythmic sound to help create the theta waves. This is a meditation that transcends time and space. This is a meditation that encourages you to connect outside the body.

For this chakra you can start by using **Akash Mudra** which consist to touch the tip of the middle finger with the tip of the thumb. Keep all other fingers straight.
Bhairava Mudra or Liberation: Rest the left hand on your lap facing upward. Lay the right hand over the left, palm facing up. Allow thumbs to touch.
Anjali Mudra or Reverence: Palm to palm, join the hands together in front of the heart center, with all the fingers touching and pointing upward.

Ascended Master:

Lord Lanto, Lord Kuthumi

Archangel:

Archangel Jophiel and Archangel Christine

Kundalini past century

Through our crown, we will realize we are one, there is no division. Below are some examples of how kundalini can be used for specific themes, such as sexuality, finances, and humanity's growth.

Sexual Kundalini:

We are one and once we are able to reach this state of connection you experience the wholeness of the universe where individuality is no longer an issue. There are no lies, no ambiguity, it's all truth instantly.

Financial Kundalini:

When humanity reaches this point in its evolution it will realize that money is completely immaterial and inconsequential since we will be able to create what we need and there will no need for advertising, money or things to fill our lives with material things since our lives will be filled spiritually.

Humanity's Kundalini:

Humanity is not there yet but it will be revolutionary when we do. However, should you want to start working your way to the fifth dimension you can start by reading the Telos Trilogy.

Chapter 14: Soul Star Chakra

This chakra is where we receive enlightenment, transcendence, and communicate with the cosmic consciousness and connect with our soul.

Basics of the Soul Star Chakra

Location	It is located a few inches above the crown chakra
Energy	**YIN/YANG** balanced
Element	**Quantum**
Mantra	Ari or We are one
Sound	C# note
Organs	Not applicable
Spine	Not applicable
Endocrine System	Not applicable
Color	Gold

The Main Functions:

It is where we access our higher purpose or our soul's destiny. It also allows you to access your soul contract and discover which archetypes are guiding your journey in this present incarnation. This is the place from which you can remove your blockages and live the life you had dreamed for yourself.

Unbalanced Chakra

This chakra is not unbalanced but disconnected. It is located outside the body and is always full of energy, but the circulation of the energy and the Crown Chakra might be cut. Consequently, the two chakras must be aligned so that the energy may freely move from one to another.

Physical:

Tired, lack of energy or motivation

Etheric:

This is where the aura emanates from, it may be leaking. You may lose the access to your connection to your soul and then we lose our direction and the reason why we were incarnated on earth.

Mental:

Depression, suicidal, mid-life crisis

Emotional:

Feeling lost or hollow, frustrated

Spiritual:

Searching for the answer to why are we here?

Healing Your Soul Star Chakra

To start, you can simply engage in an exercise that reinforces the aura through breathing, and consciously engage in absorbing light in your body. This might be a good time to see an energy healer.

Aroma therapy:

Ginger, frankincense, lavender, myrrh, orange, rosemary, thyme, white fir, ylang-ylang.

Food:

Prana energy you can also look up breatharian

Rocks & Crystals:

Based on Color:

Blue Opal, Clear Quartz, Diamond, Opal, Opal Aura Quartz, Petalite, Quartz,

Rutilated Quartz, Selenite, White Calcite

Frequency:

Angel phantom quartz, Anhydrite, Black Onyx, Black Tourmaline, Cavansite, Charoite, Chlorite Phantom, Chrysocolla, Cinnabrite, Desert Rose, Dioptase, Epidote, Galaxyite, Golden Danburite, Golden Healer Quartz , Hemimorphite, Labradorite, Larimar, Lemurian, Lemurian Jade, Lepidolite, Lodolite, Malachite, Moldavite, Moonstone, Morganite, Mystic Merlinite, Nuummite, Peridot, Pink Opal, Snowflake Obsidian, Sugilite, Super Seven, Tanzanite, Tibetan Quartz, Titanium Rainbow Aura Quartz

Yoga:

- Laying on the back (shavasana)

- Frontal laying with blocks under shoulders and forehead (modified shavasana)

Meditation:

You can use yoga breathing techniques to help you meditate, the more air you breathe in consciously the more Prana you absorb.

You have 2 Mudra options for this chakra:

Dharma Chakra Mudra or Spiritual Truth: Join the tips of the thumbs and index fingers of each hand forming a closed circle. Hands in front of the heart, touch the tips of the joined fingers together. Left palm at the bottom faces inward, right palm faces outwards.
Mani Ratna Mudra or Oneness: Bend index fingers inward and touch the tips of the index fingers to the thumbs. Join the thumbs and the hands with base of the palms touching. Extend the other fingers open.

Ascended Master:

Master St-Germain.

Archangel:

Archangel Metatron, Zadkiel and Archangel Amethyst.

Chapter 15: Foot Chakra

The foot Chakra is part of the Egyptian Chakra system where the real roots are. It an attempt to simplify the system certain important notions were lost. The feet are touching the ground, that is where our energetic roots come from and link into the earth. It helps ground our experience as Spiritual beings into the third dimension and our incarnation on earth.

Basics of the feet Chakra

Location	Through the center of the feet, not just the soles of the feet, think dimensionally.
Energy	**Yin and Yang**
Element	**Earth**
Mantra	Krim (pronounced Kreem) or I am connected
Sound	532 Hz, B note
Organs	Feet, sciatica
Spine	Feet
Endocrine System	Meridians connecting the body, nidris
Color	Magenta

The Main Functions:

To keep us grounded and to exchange energy with Mother Earth through the earth star chakra. Many times, people will refer to the base chakra as the root chakra yet, it is not so. The feet chakra is the root chakra.

The feet are an important reflection of the health of the entire chakra system. They are a main source of energy intake.

Unbalanced Chakra

This will cause people to have difficulty with their walking, balancing and mobility. It will present problems advancing in our path, problems reaching for what we want, difficulty dealing with danger, changes, a desire to lead.

Physical:

Problems can vary from the feet, ankles, Achilles heel, athletes' foot, fungus, smelling feet, to calves and leg cramping, pins and needles in the legs, sciatica nerve being pinched, hip problems, and knee issues like Kiss of Baker, water in the knee, meniscus problem, shin problems. Often getting lost or be unable to follow directions.

Etheric:

Your feet are the straight connection to past life issues that require your attention.

Mental:

Fatigued, insomnia, nightmares.

Emotional:

Restless, ungrounded, disoriented, disconnected.

Spiritual:

You are feeing lost and unable to move forward. You seem to be unable to affect change in your life.

Healing Your Foot Chakra

To start, you can simply engage in walking barefoot, look after your feet, keep them warm, don't wear constricting shoes, have a foot bath with salts in the water or a pedicure. It is also a great time to declutter your home, start with one room at a time and clear what you no longer need, release your fear that you might need it someday and let it go to a good will organization or a friend or simply throw it away.

Aroma therapy:

Lavender, lemon, roman chamomile, rosemary, vetiver.

Food:

Any root food such as beet, carrot, ginger, malanga, radish, rutabaga, turnips, etc.

Rocks & Crystals:

Based on Color:

Black Jasper, Blue Kyanite, Dalmatian Jasper, Hematite, Mahogany Obsidian, Pietersite, Tibetan Quartz

Frequency:

Apache Tear, Atlantisite, Auralite 23, Black Banded Agate, Black Kyanite, Black Obsidian, Black Sapphire, Black Tourmaline, Carnelian, Champagne Aura Quartz, England Fairy Stone, Erythrite, Fire Agate, Gold Quartz, Grey Jasper, Jet, Mahogany Obsidian, Moss Agate, Mystic Topaz, Rainbow Onyx, Opal, Picasso Marble, Red Jasper, Ruby, Rutile, Sardonyx, Serpentine, Shaman Stone, Staurolite, Sulfur, Tiger Eye, Tiger Iron, Titanium Rainbow Aura Quartz, Tourmalinated Quartz

Yoga:

any standing balancing position such as:

• Tree • Vrksasana
• Dancer • Natarajasana
• Half-moon pose • ardha chandrasana
• Warrior 3 • Virabhadrasana
• Balancing squat • Prapadasana
• Eagle pose • Garudasana
• Hand to big toe pose • Attitha padangustasana
• Side plank • Vasistasana
• Balancing table • Dandayamna Bharmanasana
• Upward facing forward fold • Urdhva Mukha Paschimottanasana
• Angle pose • Konasana

The 13th chakra system of ancient Egypt

Meditation:

Reflexology is an excellent method to circulate energy, you may use the following Mudra:

Bhu Mudra or Grounding: extend the index and middle fingers downward to make inverted V-Shaped peace signs with both hands. Curl the pinky and ring fingers inward toward the palms and place thumbs on fingertips lightly. Extend arms and bring the tips of the middle and index fingers into the ground or tops of the thighs.
Adhi Mudra or Calming: Open hands wide, tuck thumbs in to the center of the palms. Curl the fingers loosely around the thumbs, making soft fists with both hands. Rest hands palm down on thighs.

Ascended Master:

St-Francis of Assisi

Archangel:

Archangel Haniel and Archangel Joy

Chapter 16: Earth Grounding Chakra

As I mentioned throughout the book, this is a play your Soul has entered willingly, a massive stage where each individual is the Hero to their own story but interweaved into dozens or even hundreds of stories for a small appearance to major recuring roles. This incarnation in the 3rd dimension on earth inside a human body is a chance to grow and learn important life lessons to become a divine co-creator with the Universe. In order to do so , you must remember your Divine spark but also you must be fully incarnated on earth by linking to the earth energy. We are all connected and through her benevolence, the earth is helping us ascend to the fifth dimension with her. In order to do so, we must grow together and stay connected.

Basics of the Earth grounding Chakra

Location	Located between a foot and a half to three feet below the surface of the ground.
Energy	Yin
Element	Earth
Mantra	Ohm
Sound	498 Hz. A note
Color	Scarlet and/or brown

The Main Functions:

Located outside of the human body, it is accessible through the feet. It brings energy from the center of mother earth and stores it until it can connect to the human when they open their feet chakras. This is the place to connect with Mother Earth grounding us to the earth, our environment and allows us to send her gratitude because she transmutes energy until it is positive again and can be used again.

Earth is a divine being that requires our respect and as a complete entity must be respected. The concept requires a spiritual maturity that takes time to learn, understand and develop. When you connect to your earth grounding chakra you feel secure, protected, grounded and you have a wider perspective of the situation. This helps your etheric health body.

Unbalanced Chakra
This creates an imbalance in your life, instability in life, in your jobs, lodging, in relationships.

Physical:

Bone marrow-related issues. It can also play a role in any DNA-related or hereditary issues. It also governs the functioning of the lower part of the body such as legs, knees, hips and ankles.

Etheric:

These are directly related to roots growing out of the feet and linking us to the earth star chakra.

Mental:

Feeling spacey, unable to focus, irresponsible use of resources, not recycling, no respect for the environment, suffer from phobias.

Emotional:

Not being connected, unable to settle anywhere, never feeling at home anywhere.

Spiritual:

Selfish behavior that makes the person entitled to everything and a lack of trust that there is enough for everyone, hoarding, accumulation of wealth at the expense of others in fear of lack.

Healing Your Earth Grounding Chakra

To start, you can simply engage in being out in nature. You must spend time in nature, walking, gardening, listening to running water or birds singing or go by the ocean and swim in water or listen to the waves.

Aroma therapy:

Birch, cypress, juniper berry, marjoram, peppermint, white fir, wintergreen,

Food: Same as feet chakra

Rocks & Crystals:

Based on Color:

Aragonite, Black Jasper, Black Kyanite, Black Obsidian, Black Tourmaline, Chiastolite, Chlorite Phantom, Dalmatian Jasper, Hematite, Mahogany Obsidian, Smokey quartz, Schalenblende, Shaman stone, Shungite, Staurolite, Stromatolite, Tibetan Quartz

Frequency:

Atlantisite, Auralite 23, Carnelian , Champagne Aura Quartz, England Fairy Stone, Erythrite, Fire Agate, Galaxyite, Gold Quartz, Green Apophyllite, Jet, Lemurian Jade, Moonstone, Mount Shasta Serpentine, Nuummite, Red Jasper, Rutile, Septarian, Titanium Rainbow Aura Quartz, Tourmalinated Quartz, Vanadinite

Yoga:

Same as feet yoga, especially tree pose.

Meditation:

See roots grow out of your feet and connect to the earth star chakra and see the energy move from the star to your feet and then back into the star.

During your meditation you have 2 choices of mudras:

Shanka Mudra or Reassurance: Grasp the left thumb with the right hand. Curl the left hand over the right hand. Touch the tip of the right thumb to the tip of the left index, middle and ring finger. Relax the shoulders and belly and find your natural breath.

Yoni Mudra or Opening: Place the palms of the hands together with the fingers and thumbs pointing up. Interlock the pinky, ring and middle fingers downward. Bring the thumbs towards the body and join the pads of the index fingers together to form a diamond shape. Rest the hands, thumbs facing upward in front of the pelvis.

Ascended Master:

Lady Sophia

Archangel:

Archangel Raziel and Archangel Chokhmah

CONCLUSION

The best way to be good at what methods you choose to use, is to continue to practice, practice and practice more. I have been teaching the methods with hundreds of people and they in turn have been helping uncounted numbers of people. Life won't stop presenting you with opportunities to grow but now you have tools to gracefully go through your life lesson and grow into a spiritually grounded individual living life in accordance to the soul contract you originally had designed.

Each new experience allows me to delve deeper and heal all past relationships, experience completely and move into a better place surrounded with like-minded individuals who are supportive, loving and caring.

We are all one, you can have as much God source energy as you need and then channel it through your body to the world, other beings and the planet. Follow your soul purpose, be honest with your words, thoughts and actions. You are in a constant state of change and learning. There are no mistakes just lessons needed to be learned. The third dimension is only a place to learn. Once you can lift the veil of fear and free yourself, your light will shine through the veil to the rest of creation. You are important and you matter, please share your gifts, your smile and your love. Remember you are not alone, you always are with your higher self, and you can call on any Archangel or Ascended master for help.

If you wish to learn more, please visit my website : www.sonyaroy.com for a complete listing of courses and healing services available.

Other books by the same author:

Tinay the warrior princess is a series built on the ideology that Atlantis survivors escaped through space and established a colony on different planets. When they rebuilt their civilization, they decided to move the power from a man and distribute it equally to 3 women: A Seer, a Healer and a Keeper of the word. These 3 women can further extend their gifts by teaming up with each other. The seer Paletis feeling superior and undermined by the other 2 decided to eliminate them and rule alone. The precarious position she has been in has thrown society into chaos and many innocents have suffered under her rule. It is up to our Heroine to battle to find the truth and bring balance once again.

The Initiation book 1

Mani, a Canadian librarian, tells of how, many years ago, the people of Atlantis were forced to leave the earth to establish a colony in space to escape annihilation. They eventually settled on the isolated planet of Sasgorg. After several millennia of peace, the Evil Queen took control and destroyed the balance between good and evil. Fifty years under her rule has passed, and the very survival of the last of the descendants of Atlantis is threatened. Their destiny rests on the unknowing shoulders of Tinay, a young Atlantean. She must undergo the traditional rite of passage to become an apprentice artisan while unwittingly being trained to become a warrior. Tinay's destiny is to overthrow the Evil Queen and restore to her people, but is a fourteen-year-old up to the task?

NOW AVAILABLE
Soft cover ISBN 978-1-5035-2713-3
E-book ISBN 978-1-5035-2712-6

The Apprentice Book 2

Tinay is now a fifteen-year-old girl and is starting her apprenticeship as an artist on the Atlantis survivor colony planet Os. Separated from her family, she discovers how the evil queen's decisions have led society to disaster. She witnesses poverty, hunger, diseases, along with the privileged and gluttons. She gets her first glimpse of the evil queen. She will be in contact with the members of the resistance, innocently at first, and caught in the dilemma to watch from the sidelines or to join in. She needs to figure out what she will fight for, whom she will side with. She is conflicted on determining what is right, wrong, or the acceptable gray area. Her confusion reaches a new height after she learns her friend is condemned to death for reading a controversial poem that supports the resistance. She decides that should he die, his poem should be heard, and she takes her first step as a member of the resistance. Tinay will need to dig deep and help those she comes to know to save them from a horrible fate. She'll help heal the queen's victim, but is she strong enough to restore balance?

NOW AVAILABLE
Soft cover ISBN 978-1-5035-3720-0
E-book ISBN 978-1-5035-3721-7

Coming Soon:

The Artist Book 3
Tinay purses her adventure and learning in her healing gifts and trying to still develop her art abilities, and her identity quests. Available November 2019

The 13th chakra system of ancient Egypt

Spiritual Transformation of a human
Autobiography of Sonya Roy that relates to her life and her spiritual evolution. Now available on Amazon!

About Sonya Roy

Sonya Roy is a metaphysical lecturer and teacher and author of numerous books including the Tinay warrior Princess series. Her works have been translated in French and English. Since the beginning of her career as a Psycho-Educator and a teacher, Sonya has assisted people in discovering and using the full potential of their own creative powers for personal growth and self-healing. Sonya is the owner and operator of the Redu Wellness Institute, that offers classes, courses, workshops and healing sessions that contribute to the healing of the community, one person at a time.

REFERENCES

- Ascension test at www.blueskywaters.com

- "REIKI Shamanism" by Jim Pathfinder Ewing,   printed by Findhorn Press 2008

- "Shamanism for Beginners" by James Endredy printed by Llewellyn Publications 2014

- "The Celestine Vision" by James Redfield , Warner books 1997

- The Celestine Prophecy" by James Redfield, Warner books, 1995

- "The Tenth Insight" by James Redfield, Warner books, 1996

- "The Secret of Shambhala, in search for the eleventh insight" by James Redfield, Warner books, 1999

- "Crystal Chakra Healing" by Philip Permutt, CICO Books 2008

- "A handbook of Chakra Healing" by Kalashatra Govinda, Konecky & Konecky 2002

- "The complete book of Chakra Healing" by Cyndi Dale , Dale publishing, 2009

- "Color Energy" by Inger Naess, printed by Color Energy Corporation, 1996

- "The Magdalen Manuscript" by Tom Kenyon & Judi Sion, Orb communications, 2002

- "The Secret teachings of Mary Magdelene" by Claire Nahmad & Margaret Bailey, Watkins publisher, 2006

- "The human Akash" by Kryon

- "The Indigo Children- book 1" by Kryon

The 13th chakra system of ancient Egypt

- "Kryon book 1: The End Times" by Kryon

- "Kryon book 2: Don't think like a human" by Kryon

- "Kryon book 3: Alchemy of the human Spirit" by Kryon

- "Kryon book 4: The Parables of Kryon" by Kryon

- "Kryon book 5: The Journey Home" by Kryon, by Hay house, 1997

- "Kryon book 6: Partnering with God" by Kryon

- "Kryon book 7: Letters from home" by Kryon

- "Kryon book 8: Passing the marker" by Kryon

- "Kryon book 9: The New Beginning" by Kryon

- "Kryon book 10: A New Dispensation" by Kryon

- "Kryon book 11: Lifting the veil" by Kryon

- "Kryon book 12: The twelve layers of DNA" by Kryon

- "Kryon book 13: The recalibration of humanity" by Kryon

- "The book of the death of the ancient Egyptians"

- "The book of the death of the Tibetan"

- "The lost civilization of Lemuria" by Frank Joseph, Bear & Co. 2006

- "Animal Speak, the Spiritual & Magical Powers of Creatures Great and Small" by Ted Andrews, Llewellyn publications, 2012 (42 edition)

- "The Hidden Power in Humans – Chakras and Kundalini", Paramhans Swami Maheshwarananda.

- "The Chakra Bible: The Definitive Guide to Chakra Energy", Patricia Mercier.

The 13th chakra system of ancient Egypt

- "It Is Time, Knowledge From The Other Side", by Carolyn Molnar.

Printed in Great Britain
by Amazon

32224708R00067